BUYING THE EXPERIENCE

JEFF SHORE

WITH AMY O'CONNOR & RYAN TAFT

BUYING THE
EXPERIENCE

REAL LIFE LESSONS ABOUT THE WAY
REAL PEOPLE BUY HOMES

BESTSELLING AUTHOR OF *THE 4:2 FORMULA*

ISBN: 978-0-9884915-1-9

Cover design by Six Penny Graphics

Shore Consulting books are available at special quantity discounts to use as premiums and sales promotions or for use in corporate training programs. To contact a representative, please visit the Contact page at www.jeffshore.com.

CONTENTS

DEDICATION

To my amazing, incredible, hard-working,
fun-loving, meme-sharing family at Shore Consulting.

Ali Westbrook, Amy O'Connor, Ashlee Nelson,
Cassandra Grauer, Emily Leonard, Kevin Shore,
Ryan Taft and Wade Mayhue

Take a victory lap, y'all!

ABOUT THE AUTHORS

ABOUT JEFF SHORE

 Few sales leaders possess more extensive experience—and irresistible enthusiasm—than Jeff Shore. A voracious student of life and self-proclaimed sales "junkie," Jeff believes that sales is a noble profession and that salespeople who act in the best interest of their customers provide a valuable service to society.

Today, Jeff provides sales strategy and training for sales organizations internationally, working with both executive and sales teams alike. Continually pressing for new levels of personal and professional performance, he delivers hard-hitting experiences that electrify teams with quick-witted humor, personal challenges and relentless positivity.

A member of the exclusive National Association of Speakers' Million Dollar Speakers Group, Jeff is also author of four books, including *The 4:2 Formula: Getting Buyers Off the Fence and Into A Home*. His most recent book, *Be Bold and Win the Sale: Get Out of Your Comfort Zone and Boost Your Performance*, is available from McGraw-Hill Professional.

jeff@jeffshore.com |Twitter: @jeffshore

ABOUT AMY O'CONNOR

Amy brings a decade's worth of industry experience and knowledge to her impactful and enlightening seminars. Her audiences describe her infectious energy, passion and positivity as "exciting", "motivating", and "captivating".

Working hand-in-hand with a majority of the top ten homebuilders in North America—as well as private and regional builders—Amy offers a wealth of real-world expertise managing, coaching and motivating sales professionals.

Amy holds a Masters Degree in Organizational Communication from Wake Forest University and is a recognized member of the National Speaker's Association.

amy@jeffshore.com |Twitter: @amygoconnor

ABOUT RYAN TAFT.

As the former National Sales Training Manager for a $10B Fortune 100 organization and a licensed Realtor® in Arizona, Ryan Taft is consumed with a passion for helping others achieve breakthrough results in sales, business and life.

With a career spanning two decades training and coaching sales teams from call centers to Realtors®, Ryan combines his knowledge of human performance, psychology and sales skills development to deliver extraordinarily engaging, energizing and insightful training experiences that drive peak performance at all levels.

Ryan is a member of the National Speaker's Association and a frequent contributor to leading industry publications.

ryan@jeffshore.com |Twitter: @rgtaft

ACKNOWLEDGMENTS

I have a profound distaste for theory books that are not thoroughly field-tested; I certainly have no desire to contribute to that collection. And so I wish to thank the clients of Shore Consulting who have not only heard the message but have transformed their own presentations. Instruction is worthless without application. Hats off to our extended family members for their willingness to strive for great experiences.

Of course, someone of immense ability has to be out there working with real estate professionals in the role of teaching, coaching and inspiring others to apply what they learn. I have two such "someone's" in Amy O'Connor and Ryan Taft. Their contributions to this book go far beyond the messages you will see in the pages to follow. Amy and Ryan are the ones who led the charge to implement the principles of *Buying the Experience* with our clients. I am exceedingly blessed to have two of the best trainers on the planet on my staff, transforming the real estate industry with both *The 4:2 Formula* and the *Buying the Experience* messages.

Crafting a book is not simply a matter of writing 50,000 or so words. This is an enormous project, and someone needs to play the role of quarterback. That would be Wade Mayhue, Executive Vice President of Shore Consulting. At every step of the process—from concept to outline to text to layout to marketing....Wade has been both the engine and the steering wheel.

One of the problems with writing a book is that those thoughts that are crystal clear in your head sometimes miss the mark by the time they reach the paper. That is where a creative editor can work wonders. Enter June Steckler. June is an artist, both with a paintbrush and a word processor. If you enjoy the flow of the text, you can thank June for that.

Thanks to Nancy Bach for her exceedingly capable line editing skills. And to Deb Tremper for an outstanding job on layout and cover design.

And THANK YOU for your willingness to serve your customers by creating truly wonderful experiences. YOU can change someone's world today!

INTRODUCTION

THE HOME BUYER'S EMOTIONAL JOURNEY

People don't want to buy a house. They want to fall in love.

Sappy? Perhaps.

True? Absolutely.

Think about the home you live in right now. Do you remember the exact moment you walked through the door for the first time? If so, your "emotional altitude" was likely sky high (even though you may have hidden that fact from the salesperson—we'll get to that later).

Many people remember the "love at first sight" memories they have of their home. Whether you can remember the first time you laid eyes on your home or not, we all share a profound desire to emotionally connect with the places where we live.

Buying a home is not unlike other significant emotional milestones in life: weddings, childbirth, promotions, etc. Your customer dreams of buying a home for years—sometimes he has been dreaming of it for his whole life!

Home buyers save and sacrifice. They watch countless episodes of *House Hunters*. They visit model homes with longing in their eyes and peruse Houzz. com when they should be working. They buy overpriced magazines and dog-ear the corners of every other page. The moment when their dreams become a reality should be an emotional highlight of their entire lives.

Introducing a prospective buyer to her ideal home can be a truly extraordinary experience: watching her fall in love during that first encounter, helping her imagine where furniture will go, discussing décor, and envisioning parties, holidays, and the normal events that make up daily life. As salespeople, we have an incredible opportunity to experience all of this dream-turned-reality wonder over and over with excited, happy customers.

THE SAD REALITY

Alas, all too often, this does not happen.

Far too many salespeople become—to some degree—emotionally disconnected in the sales process. When walking someone through a home, they often feel unsure of what to do or say and end up talking too much or far too little. Unaware of what their customer is thinking and feeling, they lack the confidence to play the role of "assistant buyer."

It doesn't have to be this way.

When we understand the home buying experience through the eyes of our customer, we can help them write the story that is unfolding in real time, before our very eyes.

It is a cooperative tale between home buyer and salesperson. The premise is the customer's current situation; the tension increases as he considers myriad choices; the hero (that's you the salesperson!) comes to his aid with words of assistance and direction when he most needs it; and all live happily ever after.

When we understand the buying process as this kind of a story arc, the process crescendos into a purchase decision in the exciting and enjoyable way it was meant to be. (Falling in love should always be exciting and enjoyable!)

A DEMONSTRATION VS. AN EXPERIENCE

Selling a home is not easy. It takes years of work to truly master the art.

But here's the key to unlimited success in real estate sales:

Understanding how to sell is not the beginning. Understanding how a customer buys is truly the first step.

For example, you may have found that walking a customer through a home becomes an exercise in awkwardness. But when you are truly and deeply in sync with your customers, when you understand what is wrong with their lives and that you have something which will improve their current situations, everything changes.

The key to success when showing a home is to stop thinking in terms of "demonstration" and, instead, create an experience wherein you partner with your customer to begin building her future. You help her mentally try homes on for size.

You see, a demonstration is about show-and-tell. An experience is about envisioning her new life.

CHANGE IS GOOD (AND YOU HAVE A COOL JOB!)

I want to change the way you view your entire sales presentation.

You will find greater success and enjoy your job more when you master the art of helping your customers create a picture of their entire lifestyle in the context of their past, present and future experiences. You will watch this theme unfold throughout the book and hopefully it will change the way you approach your sales presentation.

This book serves as both a lesson in home buyer psychology and a how-to manual for transforming your technique. The steps we share come from decades of experience in selling both new and resale homes and in training both Realtors® and new home sales professionals around the world.

But you must understand that you do not improve by merely reading about sales theory. This is an action book, designed for application in your own presentations. You will find hundreds of sales techniques in this book, but they are all just words on a page without application.

Let me encourage you to read proactively—write in the margins, underline meaningful sentences, question the techniques, dog-ear pages. Then, rehearse specific sentences and techniques.

Do it over and over, moving past "getting it right" and practicing until you "can't get it wrong."

And one more thing: Be prepared to have some fun with this. Helping people fall in love with their future is a cool job. Lighten up, avoid the clinical behavior, and have some fun!

Do this correctly...and you will change someone's world.

SECTION ONE –

How a Customer Sees a Home

CHAPTER 1:

How We Got Here

Husband to Wife, as they approach a sales office: "Think there's a way we can ditch the salespeople?"

Wife: "No, there isn't, so just be nice."

Husband: "I'm not going to be too nice or they'll never leave us alone!"

Wife: "On second thought, maybe you shouldn't talk at all."

Husband: "The thing is, I actually <u>do</u> have some questions that I couldn't get answered on their web site, but I'm afraid if I ask anything, they'll never shut up!"

Wife: "I know, I know…Why is it always like that? Maybe we'll get the guy who doesn't even go into the model with us."

Husband: "Yeah, but that's almost just as annoying…Then they're useless. At that point why are they even there?"

Wife: "Totally. It's like, what am I supposed to do—open an upstairs window and yell down my questions to them on the porch?"

Husband: "Uh-oh…we've been spotted…one of them is coming out now…"

Wife: "OK, just don't make too much eye contact and remember, we are 'just looking'!"

REALTORS®: THE "MAKE IT UP" APPROACH

I launched my real estate career with Coldwell Banker in 1985. Their in-house orientation training was (at least at the time) state-of-the-art.

The problem then, and still a problem today, is that most Realtor® training is about business management. I learned how to farm leads, how to work the "up desk" like a champ, how to seek out referrals, and certainly how to take advantage of the swag provided me by the endless parade of lenders, title companies, termite inspectors, etc. Would you like to see my collection of vintage mortgage company key chains?

But I never learned one of the most critical sales techniques ever: how to properly walk someone through a home. I was simply left to figure it out as I went along.

The end result: My demonstration technique was as horrible as it was awkward. Was I thinking "strategy"? Not so much. It was more like *survival*—for both my customers and myself.

NEW HOMES: THE "MAP-KEY" TRAINING APPROACH

When I switched over to the new home sales world several years later, I went through a detailed program called "Map-Key" training. You might not know it by that name, but let me describe the gist of it for you

> "Let our advance worrying become advance thinking and planning."
> *Winston Churchill*

and see if it sounds familiar: *"Congratulations, you're hired. Here's a map and here's a key. Try to not get us sued."*

Still no one showed me how to walk someone through a home. So, I continued making it up as I went along. In other words, the horribleness I had been inflicting on buyers continued.

Sales professionals everywhere suffer through this exact same story. Sadly, not much has changed over the years and, not surprisingly, sales demonstration technique remains one of the most neglected aspects of sales skill development.

Indisputable proof of this becomes readily apparent to anyone who spends an afternoon visiting open houses and model home communities or watches a video "mystery shop" presentation. Heck, just watch a few episodes of *House Hunters* if you want to see how *not* to do it. Painful!

FOUR PAINFULLY COMMON PITFALLS

Over the past thirty years, I have visited more new home communities and open homes than I could possibly count. (Yes, I deserve some kind of award!) The technique infractions I have personally witnessed are too numerous to count, but the most common issues are as follows:

1. **Feature Dumping:** The ridiculous and annoying practice of pointing out glaringly obvious aspects of the home, whether the customer wants you to or not. I call it the "show up and throw up" approach. It is also known as "showing and spewing," "selling is telling," and "showing is knowing." These monikers are accurate and the approach really *is* that non-glamorous and unhelpful to the customer.

AMY'S WARNING

Feature dumping sometimes appears very appealing to certain high and mighty people in home selling organizations such as the owners of the company, the regional or division presidents, or the VPs of purchasing who want to make dang sure that you highlight every (and I mean E.V.E.R.Y.) single solitary item that money was allocated to include. Your best sales job in this instance may be selling your leaders on understanding that you will absolutely highlight important features *when* they are relevant to specific buyers.

RYAN'S TWO CENTS

The sales world has endured a false teaching that I believe is the root cause of feature dumping. This teaching makes the claim: *If you are not talking, then you are not building value.* That could not be any less true. This "talk to build value" philosophy leads to a game-show style presentation where salespeople throw out a ton of features in the hopes that one or more of them will inspire the customer to purchase. I agree with the late, great business philosopher Jim Rohn, who said: *"Hope is not a strategy."*

2. **Awkward Silence:** The flipside to feature dumping is the horribly uncomfortable practice of walking through a home with a customer but saying nothing at all. You look around, you smile uncomfortably from time to time, you check your cell phone for text messages, all in silence. It begs an important question: Why is the salesperson even there if he does not add value to the process?

3. **Blatant Neglect:** To avoid the possibility of awkward silence, many salespeople take the approach of entirely removing themselves from the home-showing process: *"You go ahead and I'll just wait out here."* Over the years, I have talked with many salespeople who suggest that this is, in fact, the most respectful of all sales methodologies. From my perspective, the same question from earlier remains: Why is the salesperson even there, and if she removes herself from the sales process, what is she doing that possibly merits a sales commission?

4. **Salesperson-Centric:** The opposite of neglect is the salesperson who inserts himself way too much into the presentation by talking about what *he* likes at every turn. *"I love this entryway. I think this countertop is just gorgeous! Oh, and look at this fireplace. I would love to curl up in front of that on a cold night!"* At best, a customer is thinking *"Who cares?"* when salespeople talk like this. At worst, another two-word phrase is in their minds. (Hint: It starts with "shut" and ends with "up.")

AMY'S PRO TIP

At the beginning of your next walkthrough, take out your smart phone, find the voice recorder (I promise it has one) and record yourself for the entire time. Then, when you are by yourself, play it back. (I just heard that sigh and saw you roll your eyes all they way to the back of your head! Hey, I warned you this was a "pro" tip.) While listening (and wincing at the sound of your own voice—we all do it), tally how many times you say "me" or "I." Also keep track of how many times you refer to the buyer or his family. Compare the two tally counts. Which count is greater and by how much? 'Nuff said.

RYAN'S PRO TIP

One way to ensure that you switch from being salesperson-centric to having a customer-centric focus is to develop a skill we call "Insane Curiosity." If you discover, via Amy's pro tip above, that you are salesperson-centric, there is a good chance you need to exercise your curiosity muscles. It is human nature to be self-focused; it takes work to retrain your brain to focus on other people.

Give your curiosity muscles a regular workout by picking a different person to get insanely curious about each day. (Not necessarily your customers. You can practice on friends and family.) The better you get at asking people about themselves and their lives, the more natural it will become to do so with your customers. It doesn't take that long for it to become second nature for you to ask about others vs. telling about yourself.

MOVING FROM "DEMONSTRATION" TO "EXPERIENCE"

So that's how we got here. Now what? Where do grow from here?

In a nutshell, I believe that the traditional "demonstration" is dead. It's time for us to focus on the "experience" instead.

At some point in the history of real estate sales, the traditional "demonstration" made sense. Think back to the post-World War II housing boom. The G.I. Bill made home ownership a viable option for thousands upon thousands of servicemen. The economy was booming and suburbs began to flourish.

Many of these first-time home buyers were moving from cramped urban apartments or old family farms. They actually needed a well-educated salesperson to demonstrate all the new features in these brand new homes: dedicated hot water heaters, washers and dryers, dishwashers, garbage disposals, central heating and cooling.

But let's face it, even the most basic apartments today offer all of these amenities—and probably more!

Do you really think you customer needs you to demonstrate how the garbage disposal works? Give me a break!

My friend, it's time to radically re-think our approach to how we walk someone through a home.

Let's look briefly at the fundamental difference between a "demonstration" and an "experience":

Demonstration	Experience
An act of showing someone how something is used or done.	*The process of doing and seeing things and of having things happen to you.*

Are you in the least bit guilty of showing a home by focusing on how things work? By focusing on what features are included in the home? By pointing out the minutiae and missing the big picture?

If so, it's time to elevate your thinking.

UNDERSTANDING THE TWO TYPES OF EXPERIENCES

This book will take you on a journey that equips you with the tools to create two specific types of experiences for your customer:

Emotional Experience: Transcends the rational/physical attributes of the home (quality, price, size) to create feelings about the home itself.

Sensory Experience: Connects one or more of the key physiological senses to the physical attributes of the home.

Emotional Experience	Sensory Experience
• Involves both the body and the mind	• Sight
• Unique to the individual	• Sound
• Deeply personal	• Touch
• Affects facial movements and vocal acoustics	• Movement
• Gives meaning to a situation	• Sense of Space

But to create this experience, you must first go a different journey—the journey of getting to know your customer on a deep emotional level.

BRIDGING THE RELATIONAL CHASM

The viewing of a home is one of the most exciting and important experiences in the buying process. It should be dramatic, electric, romantic even.

Home buyers (as we will see later in this book) desperately long to be emotionally engaged with the home of their dreams. They *want* to fall in love at first sight! It's a travesty that so many well-intentioned salespeople inadvertently punch love right in the face with a hackneyed and ill-conceived "demonstration".

Too many salespeople treat the "demonstration" of a home as merely another item to check off from their customer to-do list—this is why we must think in terms of and "experience" instead of a "demonstration".

So what holds us back from creating an "experience" of a home? Why do we fall into "demonstration" mode?

Frequently a relational chasm prohibits salespeople from engaging at a deep and meaningful level with their customers. When salespeople operate in this kind of emotionless mode, the entire home buying transaction is purely business. Maybe there is a part of you that thinks this all-business approach is completely acceptable.

Let me challenge that thinking with a different perspective. Suppose you were selling a home not to a client, but to your sister. What would be different? *Everything!*

Yes, everything would change. First of all, trust would already be a part of your relationship. Once you understood what she needed, you would be downright giddy to show her the home of her dreams. The process would be an enjoyable experience for *both* parties.

WHAT ARE THE KEY DIFFERENCES BETWEEN SHOWING A HOME TO YOUR SISTER AND SHOWING TO A CLIENT?

1) **Relational Foundation:** There is a comfortable trust in place with your sister.

2) **Understanding of Need:** You know what your sister requires and desires.

3) **Ease of Rapport:** The conversation flows with knowledge and helpfulness, following an emotional pacing that is both fluid and natural.

Establishing these three points as much as possible, early on in your conversations with customers will enable you to create a moving, memorable and motivating experience for your home buyer.

A FEW NOTES ON EMPATHY

Working with customers day after day can cause us, as salespeople, to become desensitized to the customer experience. In order to keep a fresh perspective and gain empathy for customers, I regularly visit new home communities and open homes.

I suggest you do the same. By going through multiple "demonstrations" with salespeople, you will have a greater understanding of how your customer feels. Remember that knowing what *not* to do is just as powerful as knowing what *to* do.

APPLICATION QUESTIONS

Take a moment to mull over these four questions. They will get you thinking about changes you need to make in the way that you show homes to your customers.

1. Is my approach based on tradition and routine or on a well-considered strategy? Can I defend each step in my presentation with a proven strategy?

2. Could I make this a lot more fun…for my customer and myself?

3. Can I commit to creating a difference in the way my customer experiences a home?

4. Can I diligently practice just one new technique today to get things started?

Based on what you have read thus far, what immediate changes will you make in your approach?

. . . .

. . . .

. . . .

. . . .

. . . .

. . . .

. . . .

. . . .

. . . .

. . . .

. . . .

. . . .

. . . .

. . . .

. . . .

. . . .

. . . .

. . . .

. . . .

CHAPTER 2:

Looking Through the Eyes of a Home Buyer

INSIDE A HOME BUYER'S MIND: "I can't believe we're going to move! I am SO excited! I feel like I have been waiting to do this for SO long. I just hope we can find what we want quickly. I know *exactly* what I want, I think. Oh man, what if we can't find what we want? I don't want to be one of those people who looks for a new place for *years*. I'm not even sure it would be worth moving if it takes that long. Surely, it won't take that long, I hope! I'm going to miss some things about this place though. We've had a lot of good times here. If I think about it too long, it seems almost wrong to leave the place where we have made so many great memories…but…I am SO excited! I can't believe we're going to move!"

A HOME BUYER'S GOALS

Contrary to the way things may appear externally to the salesperson, customers neither desire nor anticipate an elongated buying process.

They begin their house hunt with many hopes and dreams, but looking at thirty or forty homes before making a decision is *not* one of those hopes and dreams! In fact, the opposite is true.

Buyers want to fix their current problem, they want to fall in love with the solution, and they want to do it all as fast as possible.

It really is that simple. A customer is standing in front of you for one reason and one reason only: She wants to improve her life. Something about her family's current housing situation needs fixing. If she were perfectly satisfied, she would not be shopping in the first place.

Having determined that her problem is severe enough to merit uprooting her family and moving, she has two goals in regard to selecting their next home:

1) Solve the current problem
2) Fall in love during the process

Effective salespeople determine their strategy according to these two goals. They will:

3) Figure out the problem
4) Help the customer fall in love

Though admittedly not the norm, I have heard countless stories over the years of people who fell in love with the very first home they saw. Some were wise enough to move quickly. Others fell in love but were hesitant and ended up missing out on the purchase opportunity.

THE HOME BUYER AS AN EMOTIONAL BEING

Many years ago, my wife and I wanted to get a dog but we were unsure about which breed was right for us. We did a great deal of research before deciding on the Jack Russell Terrier. We thought this would be a good match for our lifestyle. (It will be helpful to understand that I have a history of both questionable choices and self-destructive behavior!)

Having done our extensive homework, we began our search to find the perfect dog. We scoured websites. We visited breeders. We went to dog shows. We talked to Jack Russell owners. We knew to look at the markings, at the length of leg, at the barrel of the chest, and at the general disposition. We were the proverbial "sophisticated buyers."

But we bought Charlie for one reason. When I held him for the first time, he licked my nose. It was all over. For all the research and all the education, after all the logic and all the analysis, we made a completely emotional decision.

That's nothing compared to what your customer goes through when deciding to buy a home. It is the biggest financial commitment of her lifetime and it involves an intricate web of details and analysis. Nonetheless, the home buyer is an emotional being who makes emotion-based choices.

This reality breeds a particular brand of conflict when it comes to viewing homes. Too often, customers believe they must analyze homes in a strict business-only mode and keep their emotions in check. They approach home viewings from the logical side of their brain, and they work hard at keeping their emotions hidden from the salesperson.

WHY DO SO MANY HOME BUYERS HIDE THEIR EMOTIONS?

So why do home buyers do this?

I believe the answer to that question is both simple and profound: They have been *trained* to do this! They learn to mirror the dry, unemotional approach of far too many salespeople. They adhere to an unspoken assumption that if they show emotion, they will be taken advantage of or misunderstood. They feel that they don't have *permission* to become emotionally engaged. It's just not what one does in such settings, as per the many professional (aka: detached) salespeople they have encountered over the years.

It is exceedingly difficult and downright uncomfortable for a buyer to exceed the emotional altitude of a salesperson. Even if a buyer feels genuinely excited and emotionally drawn to a home, if you, the salesperson, are not showing a level of emotion or excitement anywhere near a

> "Your intellect may be confused, but your emotions will never lie to you."
> *Roger Ebert*

customer's level of engagement, she will downplay her feelings. To a certain degree, buyers match the emotional tone a salesperson sets.

Consider the internal battle that rages unseen. It is very much akin to our high school days: *"Oh man…there she is…I really like her, but I have to play it cool so she can't tell!"* While entirely understandable in 10th grade, this kind of thinking is ridiculous and wholly unnecessary when it comes to home buying. In fact, it robs everyone of the joy in the process. You have the privilege and the responsibility to create a relational environment in which your customer feels safe to express his feelings about any home you show him.

All of the ingredients for your customer's fall-in-love moment might be there, but if you have not shown some emotion yourself—if you haven't set a tone of transparency—you won't get to see that magical moment because you have not earned the right to do so. You may miss out on the moment (and even the sale) because your customer doesn't believe she has permission to show you how she really feels. Don't be a "murderer of love!" (That will only make sense if you have seen the movie, *Dan in Real Life*, which I highly recommend.)

"UN-TRAINING" AND WHY HOME BUYERS HAVE MORE FILTERS THAN INSTAGRAM

Like it or not, your customer has been trained in the "art" of viewing homes. And he has been trained by his experiences with other salespeople. A norm has been established.

You see, customers are not born with genetically coded expectations about viewing homes—their "training" is completely experiential. This means we have some *un*-training to do if we want to make the process more enjoyable for our customers.

IT'S ABSURDITY, I TELL YOU!

The traditional way of showing homes is far different and drastically inferior to how salespeople demonstrate any other luxury product.

Think about it. If we are buying a car, we expect to test drive it. You know, get behind the wheel and take it for a spin on an actual road. If we are buying a wedding dress, we try it on at least once, if not several times.

But when it comes to new homes, we gingerly walk through them as if they are museums and the salespeople are tour guides. It's as if there are red velvet ropes keeping everyone out of the pristine rooms and in the very spaces where people are supposed to sleep, eat, sort dirty laundry, and shower, we salespeople gently hover.

We give educational lectures (in respectfully hushed tones) about each space and we make sure no food or soda is consumed during tours. *Stop the insanity!* Stop giving museum tours and start creating real-life enjoyment for your customers! Put your feet up, have a snack, lounge a bit...get real!

In addition to what customers learn from viewing other homes and inter-acting with countless salespeople before they meet you, they also bring their own personal experience filters to the process. As you show them a home, they cannot help but think of the home they currently live in or homes from their past.

They also mentally compare the home you are showing them to other homes they have seen in person, online, or even on television. What a customer wants and needs in a home is constantly being run through a series of filters that are wholly unique to him.

And in the case of couples, there are her filters, his filters, and their filters. That's a lot of filters! (Let's not even talk about the filters the kids, grandparents, and pets all bring with them!) If salespeople could see how many homes run through the mind of an average customer during a typical home viewing, they would find themselves utterly amazed.

Cut your customers some slack—they are processing *a lot*!

FROM THE MOUTH OF A HOME BUYER

Listen to this story from a real home buyer who was actively looking to move at the time of this writing:

> *In regard to how I was trained by the process of looking at homes: I realized early on that if I asked a single question at an open house, the Realtors®/salespeople would be over-the-top aggressive about getting me to sign their guest list/take their card. So, I stopped asking and even stopped making eye contact sometimes. My instinct was to be friendly and interested when I went to open houses and I often did have questions, but I quickly learned that being open was asking for trouble, so to speak.*
>
> *In regard to how I was trained by a Realtor®: The first Realtor® we ever worked with (buying our first home) echoed every comment I made about a house. Literally. It was like she didn't have an opinion of her own. I even tested it to see if I was imagining things and no, that's what she was doing. (Me: "I'm not sure I like this ceiling height." Our Realtor®: "Not sure about the ceiling height.") So, I started talking (revealing my emotions, thoughts, reactions) a lot less because I didn't like/need to hear her say the same thing I had just said. I <u>really</u> wanted her to bring new*

information to my comments or at the very least agree with me, not just repeat what I said.

As this relates to my search, I have a thing about the mid-century ranch house layout because I grew up in one, and have now bought and lived in two, and I swear, I never want to buy a ranch house with a narrow hall leading to two or three bedrooms EVER AGAIN! Enough already! If a property was perfect in every other way, I would probably cave, but it would definitely be a mental hurdle I would have to get past. Depending on the environment a salesperson created, I would either share this with them or not. I'd prefer to share it and process it with them, but if I had the impression that they wouldn't "get it," I would keep the hurdle to myself. I would also fear that if I told them, they would think such a thing silly, petty, or irrelevant or they might be dismissive of my strong feelings.

MEMORY VS. IMAGINATION (WHY HOME BUYERS NEED YOU!)

Your customer bases her filters on past experiences and therefore those filters reside firmly in her memory. That's a problem because the purchase decision she makes will be born out of her imagination. There is a natural psychological conflict at play, a battle between memory and imagination. Our memory draws us to the comfort of the past; our imagination propels us forward to a better future.

Here is where it gets difficult. To paraphrase Harvard psychologist Dan Gilbert, our memory is more powerful than our imagination. Every significant memory holds a significant emotion attached to it. This is typically not the case with our imagination.

It is up to the salesperson to attach a positive emotion to the customer's future experiences.

MEMORY VS. IMAGINATION

Recently, my wife Melissa took me to a health expo in Phoenix where hundreds of salespeople tried to sell us every gizmo under the sun. Melissa was particularly excited about an exercise machine that cost $800. The minute she told me about it, I flashed back to when I was a kid and my father spent $800 on an exercise contraption that ended up serving him as an outstanding clothes hanger. Without knowing anything about the machine that Melissa wanted, I vetoed the purchase.

Melissa *really* wanted this machine so she asked me to at least just visit with the woman at the booth. This woman was a pro. In short order, she had me telling her about my back issues and with that, she insisted that I use the machine right then and there to "see if I liked it." While I was trying out the machine, she asked me how long I have had back pain and what types of therapy I have tried. And then, with one short but perfect phrase—designed to attach a positive emotion to my imagination—she simply said, "What if this works?"

Needless to say, the machine is now in my house.

The memory vs. imagination battle is the primary reason why salespeople must be fully engaged in the process of showing a home.

Given all that customers are processing, they will mentally flounder if left completely on their own. They need you, an empathetic and knowledgeable salesperson, to help them engage their imaginations and create positive emotions about their future.

HOME BUYER BRAIN STRAIN

Buying a home is a creative, emotional, right-brain activity. The logical left brain is involved and fully engaged, but the right brain dominates. Buying a home also ranks among the most stressful things we do in a lifetime. Does stress reside in the logical side or in the emotional side of the brain? You got it—the emotional side.

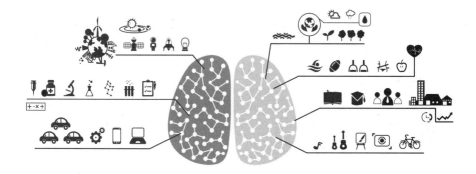

Home buyers need to make a decision from the creative right side of their brain. But they must see through the fog of stress that resides there in order to make such a decision. Cue: serious brain strain!

This is why seeing a large number of homes actually becomes detrimental to most buyers. Facing countless choices only adds to the cognitive strain by defusing the home buyer's emotional power.

When faced with too many options, the selection process becomes more of a duty than a journey. Once in this duty mode, buyers rely increasingly on the logical side of their brain. Not good.

This is how people end up buying homes they don't love. Overwhelmed by too many choices, customers relieve cognitive strain by eliminating options in an analytic, impersonal way.

When home buying becomes more about data than falling in love and realizing a dream, all the joy and humanity of the process is lost. #nothanks.

AMY'S PRO TIP FOR REALTORS®

Preview all homes *before* taking buyers to see them in order to preemptively eliminate the duds, thus minimizing the number of homes you show to a single buyer on any given day. This will greatly reduce stress and confusion. Strapping a buyer into your car at 9:00 a.m. and handing him 20 listings and a venti triple shot latte is just asking for a mental breakdown.

RYAN'S PRO TIP FOR REALTORS®

Most Realtors® simply ask what a potential home buyer is looking for and then enter those facts into MLS. Try this: Ask what your customer *doesn't* want in her next home. Since people often eliminate homes due to something they dislike about a property, it is crucial to know what the "don't wants" are at the very beginning of the process. Being equipped with this knowledge will save you and your customers an enormous amount of time.

Making the home buyer's cognitive strain even worse, humans operate with a finite capability to handle stress. At some point, we will simply give up and default to the most comfortable place our brains can find. In the case of your would-be home buyer, that means heading back to the home he is in right now. Paralysis by analysis, right? Bad news.

Great salespeople keep the home buying process as simple as possible. Your customer is already bumping up against a ceiling of complexity. This reality must be countered with a sales process that is clear, quick, and easy to comprehend.

Read on!

APPLICATION QUESTIONS

Pose the following questions to yourself as a kind of rubric for applying greater clarity and ease to your sales process:

1. In thinking back on my sales career, which transactions have been the most fulfilling and enjoyable, for both myself and my customers? Is there a common thread in them? Is that commonality the level of emotional altitude that was present in each case?

2. Do my customers show their emotional side when I take them through homes? If not, what can I do to encourage that? If so, how can I get to that point sooner in the process?

3. How can I attach more emotion to the future experience of living in a new home?

4. What can I do to ease the amount of cognitive strain my prospects experience?

Based on what you have learned in this chapter, what immediate changes will you make in your approach?

. . . .

. . . .

. . . .

. . . .

. . . .

. . . .

. . . .

. . . .

. . . .

CHAPTER 3:

Get Your Head on Straight

INSIDE A HOME BUYER'S BRAIN: "I feel like I'm going to lose my mind. There is so much to keep track of. I can't keep everything we're supposed to be figuring out about the new house in my head on top of work and the kids and regular life! I'm so scared that something is going to fall through the cracks or that we're going to go to all of this trouble and expense and not be happy with how the house ends up. I may seriously lose my mind before this is all said and done! Can I really go through with this?"

In light of the stress-ridden plight of our customers, the sales professional must maintain a clear and consistently positive mindset. Selling is a mental game and great salespeople protect their mental energy at all costs. This is not a selfish goal. Great salespeople understand that positive energy is both contagious and transferable. The process of showing a home can be filled with excitement, energy, and joy, but that all starts with the sales professional.

Let's talk about how to do that.

THE INTENT-TECHNIQUE CONNECTION

Which is more important: intent or technique? Purpose or strategy?

I contend that intent and purpose (your "why") will guide strategy and technique (your "what" and "how").

One might say that Eric Clapton is a talented guitar player, LeBron James is great at basketball, and Meryl Streep is a gifted actress because of their respective technique.

I would argue that their technique would not even exist without their intention, belief, and purpose. The conviction of purpose drives top performers to spend countless hours perfecting their craft.

Intent to excel drives the formation of effective technique.

YOUR FOCUS DETERMINES YOUR FUTURE

The author of *Rich Dad Poor Dad*, Robert Kiyosaki, shares a story which illustrates how intent guides technique and focus determines follow-through.

In the book, Robert writes about how he has been learning to drive professional racecars. (I guess that's what you do when you are a bazillionaire.) When he proved to be proficient in racing the track, Robert then learned how to avoid and handle a crash. During one such crash lesson, the instructor made Robert's car skid toward the track wall at high speed. Where do you think Robert's focus went? If you guessed the wall, you are correct. In this scenario, driving students always take their eyes and mind off the track (where they want to go) and focus on the wall (where the disaster is about to happen). It's understandable, right?

Back to Robert's experience, when a car is skidding toward a wall and a seemingly imminent crash, the instructor will physically grab students' helmets and force them to move their focus from the wall back to the track. Those instructors know that you need to be focused on what you want and where you are going...even when you are about to crash.

Keeping your mind set on the right intentions will allow your technique to flow naturally from those intentions.

> *"As he thinks, so he is; as he continues*
> *to think, so he remains."*
> **James Allen**

BELIEVE YOU MAKE A DIFFERENCE

Begin with the profound conviction that you matter to your customer. A home does not, as some would erroneously suggest, "sell itself."

- You enjoy the esteemed privilege of connecting a customer to a home, revealing how a particular home will improve his life in specific and profound ways.
- You help your customer work through any anxieties she might have.
- You give him a new perspective when he has objections.
- You find solutions to her problems.
- You lead him to a better life.

In short, you become the "assistant buyer" that your prospect so desperately needs.

MAINTAINING YOUR MENTAL GAME

In our line of work, you can be certain you will hear your share of customer complaints: homes that aren't built to expectations, closings that don't go well, final cleanings that were supposed to happen and didn't, etc.

Do yourself a favor. When complaints start to weigh heavily on you, pick up the phone and call the last few happy and satisfied homeowners you helped and check in with them to see how they are doing. Let their happiness wash over you. Feel their joy and know that you made a difference in their lives.

BELIEVE YOU HAVE A PURPOSE

Perhaps the most significant difference you can make is influencing your customers to do the right thing. You help them make a decision that is in their best interest.

Sales is not show-and-tell. Sales is about making it easy for customers to do difficult things.

The concept of persuasion has been much maligned in the sales process. Too many salespeople see persuasion as being akin to manipulation. We tend to think of it as a dirty word. (Perhaps Alec Baldwin screaming *"coffee is for closers"* comes to mind.)

> "Character may almost be called the most effective means of persuasion."
> *Aristotle*

The sales industry definitely suffers from the old-school, stereotypical image of a salesperson dressed in a plaid jacket and white shoes, sporting a shiny medallion, and wearing a toupee, trying to be "persuasive." *"What's it gonna take to get you into this house today?"* It kind of makes your skin crawl, doesn't it?

I wholeheartedly reject any such image. Persuasion is about helping the customer to make a decision that is in her best interest.

It is not at all unlike raising children or providing assistance in tax preparation or teaching someone a skill. In fact, I earnestly hope I am persuading you *right now*!

When showing homes, you are not simply walking through, pointing out features. If that is all you are doing, you are selling yourself (pun intended) short. You have the potential and the responsibility to be far more than a walking, talking brochure. The Internet can serve that purpose.

You are there to move your customer to a purchase decision. Showing a home has an end goal. If you believe in this principle, you will find that an entirely different approach is in order.

CHANGE SOMEONE'S WORLD

> *"I've learned that people will forget what you said,*
> *people will forget what you did,*
> *but people will never forget how you made them feel."*
> *~ Maya Angelou*

Ultimately, we are charged with, and given the privilege of changing the world for our customers. This is profound and important. You will literally change the lives of the people you help.

From time to time, I still drive by the first home I ever sold, a 1,200-square-foot starter home in the Irvington district of Fremont, California. I recognize that behind the door of that home live a thousand stories.

I made a difference, and for that I am proud. I hope you feel the same way.

APPLICATION QUESTIONS

Think about these three important questions as you consider your own mindset:

1. How would I define my purpose in selling?

2. How would I narrow that definition for the process of demonstrating a home?

3. Am I sometimes self-conscious or even embarrassed about my role as a salesperson? Who can I trust to discuss this issue with?

· ·

· ·

· ·

· ·

· ·

· ·

· ·

· ·

· ·

· ·

· ·

· ·

· ·

· ·

THREE TIPS TO GET YOUR HEAD ON STRAIGHT

When I was 20 years old, I knew my head wasn't on straight. I was in a rock band that was going nowhere fast. I was filled with self-doubt and wasn't looking toward the future with much hope. Honestly, I dreaded each day and began to be very negative about myself and everyone else.

Fortunately, I was introduced to a mentor who shared three tips that forever changed my life and got my head on straight. Here they are:

1. **Associate Above Your Current Thinking**
   You become like the people you hang out with. Hang out with Jeff Shore and Amy O'Connor for a while and you will raise your level of thinking! If you are hanging out with people who are negative, victim oriented, or lackluster, you need to make a change. Get around people who are on fire to win.

2. **Be a Voracious Reader**
   We have access to the most successful people in the history of the world via books. If you want to move faster toward your goals, become a voracious reader. And don't tell me you don't have time to read. Turn off the television and get your face in a book! Here are a few suggestions to start with: *As a Man Thinketh* by James Allen, *Awaken the Giant Within* by Tony Robbins, and *Think and Grow Rich* by Napoleon Hill.

3. **Control What You Listen To**
   The world is full of negativity. Turn on a radio or a TV and you will instantly hear how bad the world is. Controlling what you listen to is vital for your future success. I encourage you to make listening to inspiring leaders like Jim Rohn and Darren Hardy a part of your daily routine. Downloading podcasts and audiobooks is easy, and many are free.

> Consider replacing your daily perusal of depressing online news with a daily TED Talk viewing (YouTube and ted.com) and make it your new normal to be vigilant about protecting yourself from negative input.

Based on what you have read thus far, what immediate changes will you make regarding your mindset and your beliefs about your role as a sales professional?

. . . .

. . . .

. . . .

. . . .

. . . .

. . . .

. . . .

. . . .

. . . .

. . . .

. . . .

. . . .

. . . .

. . . .

CHAPTER 4:

The Three Commitments You Must Make

Let's review a few mental focus points of commitment before we dive into the technique side of things.

COMMITMENT #1: DO IT

Begin with a commitment. Commit to having fresh perspective and renewed energy as you walk someone through a home. You will learn techniques in the pages that follow, but for now just get your intention right. Everything else will fall into place.

One way to hold yourself accountable to the "Do It" commitment is to start tracking the frequency of your home showings. How many times are you walking someone through a home over the course of a week? Track your frequency and also what you learn, recording what goes well and what needs improvement. Think of tracking as a quest to mastery.

Increase both your intentionality and your frequency and you will improve your results. I guarantee it.

COMMITMENT #2: GET GOOD AT IT

In reading and implementing the ideas in this book, you will discover new ways of doing business. In fact, you may discover some bad habits you have developed over time. These need to be replaced by good and healthy sales habits.

It won't all be victory and satisfaction at first (skill development *never* works that way), but don't be discouraged when it doesn't go well. *Your focus should be on progress rather than perfection.* Understand that we learn much more through our failures than we do through our successes.

If you ain't failin', you ain't tryin'!

Keep in mind that this is a skill development journey and skill development takes time. Just ask Taylor Swift, Aaron Rodgers, or anyone else who is at the top of his or her game. A whole lot of practice, a whole lot of mistakes, a whole lot of blood, sweat, and tears went into getting to where they are now. Bite off little chunks of learning and aim to master specific skills. And, be patient.

> "Success is nothing more than a few simple disciplines, practiced every day."
> *Jim Rohn*

Commit right now to mastering the art of experiential selling. Nothing else, just that for now.

COMMITMENT #3: HAVE FUN WITH IT

This really should be the fun part of selling homes, for both you and your customer. You can commit right now to falling in love with watching people fall in love. Take great pride in knowing you have facilitated their love affair with their new home. (You're like eHarmony for houses!) You are changing their world, right there on the spot.

Be exciting, but feel free to be *excited* as well.

Now, let's have some fun!

APPLICATION EXERCISE

Before you move on, try verbalizing the commitment you are making to yourself. In your own words, describe the end result of your journey to experiential selling.

. . . .

. . . .

. . . .

. . . .

. . . .

. . . .

. . . .

. . . .

. . . .

. . . .

. . . .

. . . .

. . . .

. . . .

. . . .

. . . .

. . . .

SECTION TWO –

The Rules of Experiential Selling

· · · · · · · · · · · · · · · · · ·

CHAPTER 5:

Rule #1:
It's All About the Customer

TRANSFORMING YOUR VIEW OF THE SALES PROCESS

Far too many salespeople see the "demonstration" as an exceedingly boring part of the sales process. They could give house tours in their sleep. In fact, sometimes their customers think that's exactly what they're doing!

But what if we radically reframe the very nature of what we are attempting to accomplish during a "demonstration"? What if we looked at this process from an entirely new angle?

What if I were to tell you that the most important principle in showing a home is *NOT about showing the home?*

That's right, experiential selling is not about the home at all.

RULE #1:
THE "DEMONSTRATION" IS NOT ABOUT THE HOME.
IT IS ABOUT THE CUSTOMER.

I cannot stress this enough. If you change your perspective about this one thing you will revolutionize your entire approach, all for the customer's benefit. Think about it. This paradigm shift changes everything.

THE VILLAGES: A CASE STUDY

As a real estate professional, you owe it to yourself to take a trip to The Villages, the awe-inspiring active adult community in central Florida. There is no place like it in the world.

> "Nothing ever becomes real till it is experienced."
> *John Keats*

Over 100,000 people call The Villages home, all in one master-planned community that spans three counties. There are seventy restaurants and thirty golf courses, miles of trails for golf carts (the transportation mode of choice), and community and recreation centers in every neighborhood. More than 1,500 activity options for residents are listed on The Villages website every week.

Talk with any salesperson on staff at The Villages and he will tell you the same thing: It's not about the homes. Owning in The Villages is all about the lifestyle experience. The homes are fantastic, but they are not the focal point.

IT'S NOT ABOUT THE HOME

You must adopt the mindset that experiential selling is not primarily about the home, but rather about the life that your customer will have when living in it.

"Demonstration" is all about the home:

- *"Notice the tall ceilings."*
- *"Those are nice granite countertops."*
- *"Looks like they upgraded the molding."*

Experiential selling is all about the customer:

- *"Let's talk about where the piano will go in order for your family to get the most enjoyment out of it."*
- *"I know you love to cook…walk around the kitchen and imagine preparing a meal for a dinner party of eight."*
- *"Let's brainstorm how to get the most out of this incredible view."*

What is the difference between these two approaches? One is about the features of the home. The other is about how the customer will experience life in their new home.

Demonstration	Experience
An act of showing someone how something is used or done.	*The process of doing and seeing things and of having things happen to you.*

You tell me which creates greater impact. Which do you think buyers prefer?

HOUSES ARE PREDICTABLE. PEOPLE ARE NOT.

Let's face it, most homes are made up of the same core elements: a kitchen, bedrooms, bathrooms, living areas, and a garage. The elements are the same; they just vary in arrangement and size from home to home.

Not so with customers. Every person is unique. Every customer has a different use for each space in a home. Each customer is coming from a different background with different living experiences and different living expectations.

Because of this fact, discovery is crucial. This book is about engaging the customer with an incredible experience.

That experience hinges on this important principle:

There is no effective experience in the absence of effective discovery.

Don't think for a moment that you can skip discovery and still create a memorable experience.

WHY ACTIVE LISTENING IS SO IMPORTANT

I recently had some minor issues with my blood pressure so my primary care physician sent me to a cardiologist for a precautionary exam. Arriving on time, I was hustled back to a nondescript examination room, issued a designer paper gown—it opened in the front. Whoo!—and was left waiting for 30 minutes in the freezing cold room with nothing to do but thumb through outdated, hopefully uncontaminated fashion magazines.

Mercifully, the door finally swung open and in rolled Doogie Howser, M.D. I say "rolled" because that is literally what he did. He was sitting in a chair which was connected to a wheeled table with a laptop on it. I call him Doogie Howser because, at least to me, he looked to be about 16 years old. (Remember the early '90s TV show with Neil Patrick Harris playing the part of a genius whiz kid doctor?)

My Doogie never once lifted his eyes from his laptop. He began by asking me the usual questions: name, age, medical history, etc. Then, as he continued to type, he must have remembered that it's always a good idea to, you know, treat your patients like human beings. In what I perceived to be an attempt at personal connection, he asked (still with no eye contact) "Do you have kids?" I answered, "Yes, two. A five-year-old and a four-year-old." Type, type, type...more medical questions...type, type, type...

Not three minutes later, he asked again, "Have any kids?" *Seriously?* Did he just ask me that? *Again?* I'd had enough. If Doogie can't or won't listen to me about something as simple as that, then I don't want him anywhere near my vital organs! I left. And I won't be going back.

THE HOME AS A SOLUTION

The discovery process is not for determining bedroom count and square footage requirements.

Anyone can figure those things out. Heck, you can get that information from a registration card.

What we really need to discover is:

* What is the problem?
* How does the customer's life need to be improved?

You cannot provide a solution until you identify a problem. You must go deep in the discovery process, and when you do, *everything* changes.

WHY DO PEOPLE MOVE?

According to a US Census study in which 36 million people were asked why they moved between 2012 and 2013, 48 percent of people moved due to housing-related issues. Another 30 percent moved because of family reasons, 20 percent changed residences due to work-related issues, and 2 percent moved for other reasons. Do you know why *your* last customers moved? How about the customers before them? And again I say, you cannot create an effective experience without an effective discovery. Can I get an "Amen"?

In the next chapter, you will learn about uncovering the customer's mission and how doing so will enable you to create incredibly memorable experiences for your customers.

APPLICATION QUESTIONS

Ask yourself these questions as you apply Rule #1 to your presentation:

1. In the past, has my presentation been more about the home or about the customer?

2. In what ways have I succeeded at having a customer-first presentation? In what ways can I move away from a home-first presentation?

3. What creative questions can I incorporate into my presentation that will make it more customer-centered and experiential?

Write down your action commitment as a result of your answers to these questions.

CHAPTER 6:

Discover the "Why," Not the "What"

"TO" SALESPEOPLE VS. "FROM" SALESPEOPLE

Most salespeople commonly ask questions focused on WHAT a customer is moving TO. If this is your approach, it's time for a cool change.

I believe the most powerful discovery focuses on WHY a customer is moving in the first place. What are they moving FROM?

Focusing on the "from" (vs. the "to") represents the first step in thoroughly equipping yourself to solve your customer's problem.

And you can only understand the "from" when you really take time for a thorough discovery. Glossing over the discovery process forces you to make assumptions. You start shooting in the dark.

It is unnecessary, it is dangerous, and it makes you appear to care only about your own bottom line, not about your customer's needs.

THE 4:2 FORMULA FOUNDATION

If this concept sounds familiar to you, it might be because you have read my book, *The 4:2 Formula - How to Get Buyers Off the Fence and Into a Home*. That book is almost entirely about discovery, and in it I describe the many nuanced details of this process.

If you have not yet read or been trained on The 4:2 Formula, you might consider reading that book first (or listening to the audio version). *The 4:2 Formula* will give you a solid foundation of effective discovery tools. Trust me, it's a far cry from the outdated Critical Path model.

That said, the balance of Section Two (chapters six through eight) provides an overview on effective discovery, including a brief primer on The 4:2 Formula.

THE TYPICAL DISCOVERY QUESTIONS

Think about the discovery process of a typical real estate salesperson. Ryan Taft does an interesting exercise about this in his training sessions.

He states the first part of the typical discovery questions and asks the salespeople in his class to finish the query. They *always* get it right.

It goes something like this:

- *"Is this your...   first time here?"*
- *"How did you...   hear about us?"*
- *"How many...   bedrooms are you looking for?"*
- *"Did you have a...   price point in mind?"*
- *What is your...   time frame?"*
- *"Would you mind...   filling out a guest registration card?"*

Are these inquiries about what the customer is moving "to" or what she is coming "from"?

Historically, almost all discovery questions revolve around what the customer is moving "to." And they are all about the "whats" of the sale, if you will:

- What bedroom/bathroom count does he want?
- What square footage?
- What is the time frame?
- What can she afford?
- What features are most important?
- What are the "must haves"?

C'mon, admit it—you've been trained to ask this stuff, right? And I'm sure we can agree that every single item on this list is about what the customer is moving "to" and gives very little insight into what prompted them to start looking in the first place.

It's a formulaic checklist, plain and simple. Ugh. It's the same checklist that will make you sound like every other salesperson

Great discovery (vs. checklist-style "discovery") leads us to an understanding of what the customer is moving "from." And that "from" information provides vital clues as to the reason your customer is moving in the first place.

> "The greatest obstacle to discovery is not ignorance—it is the illusion of knowledge."
> *Daniel J. Boorstin*

In fact, what the customer is moving "to" is dictated by what he is coming "from." I want to know why he is moving. I want to know what's wrong with the home he is in now. I want to know what kind of history and expectations he brings with him from his current home. I want to know who has a stake in the home buying decision—who has a voice in the conversations I have with him.

I NEED to know what is so out of sorts in his life that the only reasonable solution is for him to uproot and start over in a new place.

I make this audacious promise to you:

If you get to know your customers well enough, they will literally show you how to sell them a home.

Let me say that again. If you get to know your customers well enough, they will show you how to sell them a home.

The sales path will roll out right in front of you.

A CASE STUDY IN BEING A "TO" SALESPERSON

I was in a new home sales office near Austin, Texas where I had the opportunity to eavesdrop on this conversation between a prospective buyer ("B") and a new home salesperson ("S").

S: "Welcome. Is this your first time here?"

B: "It is."

S: "Well, thanks for stopping by. Let me ask you a few questions so I can point you in the right direction."

B: "Okay."

S: "How many bedrooms are you looking for?"

B: "At least four. Well…three and a place for a hobby room."

S: "Okay. And do you have a square footage range in mind?"

B: "At least 3,000 square feet."

S: "Got it. Are you working within a specific price range?"

B: "We're pre-qualified up to $450,000, but we need to sell our home first."

S: "Fair enough. Anything else you need to have in the home?"

B: "Well, it needs to be a one story. We would like to put in a pool and we want something with a large great room for entertaining."

S: "Great. Let's go take a look. I'll show you what I've got."

And with that, the two of them walked out to look at a model home.

Take a moment and analyze that discovery. How effective was it?

The salesperson asked some good questions, didn't she? And the questions resulted in helpful answers. All good, right?

Now take a deeper look and ask this question: Was this conversation about what the customer is moving *from* or about what the customer is moving *to?* The answer is obvious.

The fundamental flaw here is that the salesperson knows a whole lot of the *what*, but absolutely nothing about the *why!*

She left a number of important points unaddressed. Brainstorm with me on what we could otherwise discover here:

- Why is this customer thinking about moving in the first place?
- Why does he believe his current home doesn't work anymore?
- Why does he need at least three bedrooms? Who will be living in the home?
- Why does he want a hobby room? It was important enough for the customer to bring it up, so what is the hobby? Does he have a hobby room now? If not, why is that a problem?
- Why did the customer arrive at that particular square footage target? How does that compare with the size of his current home?
- Why does he need to sell his home first? And does he really *need* to, or is that his preference?
- Why does he need to have a one story?
- Does he have a pool now? Is this a need or a want?
- How does he define "great room" and what type of entertaining does he do?

The next day, I talked with the salesperson I overheard and I discovered some very interesting facts about that buyer.

He is married with three children. His girls are extremely active and love to have friends over (large great room). He also has a son who is both physically and mentally disabled (one story and a pool for exercise). His son loves to watch model trains (hobby room). They've been trying to make do with the two-story home they are in but have reached the point where they are completely weary of trying to make their current home work when it just simply doesn't suit their family's needs and lifestyle (need to sell their home).

Now, here's the twist. Our salesperson found out all of this information *after she showed him a home.*

Imagine the vibrant, fulfilling, and memorable experience she might have created if she discovered this information upfront.

She could have bonded emotionally with her customer and helped him imagine an amazing and transformational life for his family in this perfectly tailored new home.

As it was, she only discovered the most basic information and she had no choice but to "demonstrate" the home via a series of feature dumps.

And here's the bottom line: she didn't get the sale.

A FINAL THOUGHT ON DISCOVERY

Let me be very, very clear: This discussion is NOT about effective discovery. Here's the real takeaway:

You must USE what you learn about your customer during the discovery to create a richly tailored lifestyle experience of the home.

An effective discovery only helps you if use it to build an emotionally centered experience of the home for your customer.

It's time for you to think through both the nature and the depth of your early questioning habits because they lay the foundation for the entire customer experience you are about to create.

It's time to stop thinking about "to" and start focusing on "from."

APPLICATION QUESTIONS

Ask yourself these questions as you apply Rule #2 to your presentation:

1. Am I a curious person? Is that apparent in my early discovery questions with customers?

2. How much do I believe I need to know about what a customer is coming from? Is that important to me?

3. What are some key questions that will lead me to discover what a customer is coming from?

4. Am I committed to frequently saying, "Tell me more about that," or some other statement that enables my customer and me to go deeper?

Take a moment and write down a commitment about improving your discovery skills:

. . . .

. . . .

. . . .

. . . .

. . . .

. . . .

. . . .

. . . .

. . . .

. . . .

. . . .

. . . .

. . . .

. . . .

. . . .

. . . .

. . . .

. . . .

. . . .

. . . .

. . . .

. . . .

. . . .

. . . .

. . . .

. . . .

. . . .

. . . .

. . . .

. . . .

. . . .

. . . .

. . . .

. . . .

. . . .

. . . .

. . . .

. . . .

. . . .

CHAPTER 7:

The Four Things You Must Know

BECOMING A "FROM" SALESPERSON

Knowing that what a customer is coming *from* is more important than what she is moving *to*, it is wise to adopt a system of discovery which reveals the most important aspects of a prospect's situation.

Top sales professionals follow a pattern of proven questions that are strategic in nature and yet conversational in tone.

In this day and age, customers simply lack the patience to be questioned at length by a salesperson. Therefore, it is best to keep your questions limited and extremely relevant. (Think: quality over quantity.)

In addition to brevity, a comfortable, normal tone is also crucial. By "normal" I mean your regular speaking voice. Too many salespeople *put on* a "sales voice" for customers. Just don't.

You need to practice your discovery questions thoroughly (i.e., more than you think) so you can deliver them in a casual and comfortable manner. Aim for *conversing with* your customers vs. *interrogating* or *presenting to* them.

Basically, you need to ask deep, meaningful questions in a very easygoing, friendly way, right off the bat. This is a unique type of conversation and not one that will come naturally to most people.

So, PRACTICE!!

FOUR THINGS YOU MUST KNOW ABOUT YOUR CUSTOMER

Over the past thirty years I have distilled all of the initial discovery questions down into four categories. These are the areas of discovery that are critical to your being able to provide a positive, compelling experience for your customer.

> "I remind myself every morning: Nothing I say this day will teach me anything. So if I'm going to learn, I must do it by listening."
> *Larry King*

1. **Motivation**. Why is he moving in the first place? This is the single most important piece of information you need to know. Learn it early, but also learn it deeply. Be prepared with follow-up questions: "Tell me more…"

2. **Current Dissatisfaction**. Everyone moves for the same reason: a desire to improve his or her life. What does this specifically mean for your prospect? What's wrong with the home she is in now, and in what ways does she need to make things better? What are the pain points? What is she putting up with now that she really doesn't like?

3. **Future Promise**. This is all about learning what your customer is picturing in his mind. What are his hopes and dreams for life in his new home? What are the "must haves" and what are the "would likes"? What does a better life look like to him, not in terms of features, but in terms of experience?

4. **Family / Stakeholders**. Who has a say in this decision? Whose interests are being represented? Who do you need to please in the process of showing a home? (Hint: They may not always be present!)

You will find a more detailed analysis and several examples of these discovery questions in my book, *The 4:2 Formula: Getting Buyers Off the Fence and Into a Home*.

THE IMPORTANCE OF TAKING NOTES

I highly recommend taking notes during the discovery process (and throughout your entire sales presentation for that matter).

Notes are important for so many reasons: 1) Note-taking sends a message to the customer that she is important to you. 2) Note-taking is a listening skill; if you are writing, you are not talking. 3) There is no way you will be able to remember everything the customer says—why risk forgetting something and having him think, "Oh, she wasn't listening to me!" 4) As Jeff already mentioned, the discovery process is when your buyer outlines how you can sell him a home. So, this is your golden opportunity to write a step-by-step, customized selling guide. 5) Notes serve as a follow-up handbook, helping you know and remember specific details about connecting with your customer.

Note-taking can feel uncomfortable at first. There is an art to taking notes while still maintaining a conversation. Practice taking notes during conversations outside of work to accelerate your mastery of this skill!

I can confidently say that if you cover these four categories in the early stages of discovery, you will be well equipped for creating powerful customer experiences.

In his book, *The 7 Habits of Highly Effective People: Powerful Lessons in Personal Change*, the great Stephen R. Covey wrote, "Most people do not listen with the intent to understand; they listen with the intent to reply." Similarly, many salespeople do not discover with the intent to understand, they discover with the intent to sell. When discovery becomes fully about the customer—her motivation, what she is moving from and what she desires to move to—*then* you are well positioned to execute an effective and powerful experience for your buyer.

THE IMPORTANCE OF ASKING BETTER QUESTIONS

When communication fails, most people blame the other person for the breakdown. *"He just doesn't get me!"* or *"That girl is all over the map. It's so hard to understand her."* Psychologists call this phenomenon "attribution theory." In short, the theory is that we all tend to think: If it goes well it's because of me. If it goes poorly it's because of someone else.

What if instead, **you** took responsibility for **both** sides of communication? Taking responsibility for both sides ensures that you communicate clearly and effectively. If I am talking with someone and I don't understand what he or she means, it is up to me to gain clarity by asking better questions. If that same person doesn't understand what I am saying, then I need to use more descriptive words, paint clearer pictures, or use better analogies.

So how do you know if you are a great communicator? An easy way to tell if you need to adjust how you communicate is to pay close attention to how your customers tend to respond to you. A poor response can usually be traced back to a poor question. Lack of understanding on the part of a customer can often be caused by a salesperson using confusing or mundane words. If you sense that customers aren't responding well to your discovery questions, work on making them more effective. As Jeff said, when you get the discovery right, it will set you up to provide a fantastic experience for the customer!

APPLICATION EXERCISE: CREATE YOUR OWN CASE STUDY

Think of the last time you purchased a home or about the buyers to whom you most recently sold a home.

Now look at the four categories listed above and ask yourself, "Would a crystal clear understanding of each of those subjects have made a significant impact on the quality of the customer experience?"

There are other topics to discover, of course (financial capability, shopping experience, etc.), but when you start with the most strategic categories first, you will find that the rest of the necessary discovery will happen naturally.

Take some extended time now to write in your own words the way you would phrase questions that would help you learn about each of the four categories from a specific customer. Keep your wording and tone conversational, making sure your questions don't sound like an interrogation. Read the questions out loud to see if they pass the "real life" test (you don't want to sound like you're reading from a script).

Keep tweaking your writing and reading out loud until your questions sound and feel like your natural self. Feel free to do this in a public setting…it could be highly entertaining for those around you!

. . . .

. . . .

. . . .

. . . .

. . . .

. . . .

. . . .

. . . .

. . . .

. . . .

. . . .

. . . .

. . . .

. . . .

. . . .

. . . .

. . . .

. . . .

. . . .

. . . .

. . . .

. . . .

. . . .

. . . .

. . . .

. . . .

. . . .

. . . .

. . . .

. . . .

. . . .

. . . .

. . . .

CHAPTER 8

The Buying Formula

HOW HOME BUYERS MAKE PURCHASE DECISIONS

I teach to my clients a proven formula by which customers make purchase decisions. This equation explains exactly why people purchase. It also reveals where they get stuck.

The Buying Formula is comprised of three factors:

1. **Current Dissatisfaction**

    As mentioned in the previous chapter, every customer comes to you with some degree of dissatisfaction in his current home and, therefore, in his life. When people feel perfectly pleased with their home, they do not shop for a new one.

    > "The little dissatisfaction which every artist feels at the completion of a work forms the germ of a new work."
    > *Berthold Auerbach*

    Think of the last time you went shopping for a new mattress. There was a motivating dissatisfaction, correct? Exactly.

    Current Dissatisfaction operates as a powerful motivator. Moreover, it creates an important primer for buying: urgency.

    You will want to highlight, underline, print, and post, perhaps get a tattoo of this next statement:

The single greatest predictor of urgency is dissatisfaction.

I cannot stress this strongly enough. The single greatest predictor of urgency is dissatisfaction. The higher the dissatisfaction, the greater the urgency. Period.

2. **Future Promise**

In addition to Current Dissatisfaction, the customer creates a picture of hope in her mind. We call this "Future Promise."

Future Promise creates a vision where the home buyer sees herself living in her new home and community. It's the promise of things to come and it represents her improved life.

You may encounter customers who, at first, do not appear to suffer a raging Current Dissatisfaction. Here's the interesting thing—when you effectively discover the customer's "why" and then share a compelling Future Promise, their Current Dissatisfaction suddenly rises.

It's like going for a spin in a friend's brand new car and suddenly realizing all the shortcomings of your own ride.

3. **Cost + Fear**

Current Dissatisfaction and Future Promise create strong motivations to buy, but they run up against an equally strong inhibiting factor: Cost and Fear.

> "The cost of a thing is the amount of what I will call life which is required to be exchanged for it, immediately or in the long run."
> *Henry David Thoreau*

The financial Cost and Fear (perceived or actual), combined with the hassle of the process, the consequences of making a poor decision, fear of salespeople, etc. all work *against* a home buying decision.

You may encounter a customer with a scorching Current Dissatisfaction and a compelling Future Promise, but if the home he desires sits $200,000 over his price range, you consequently face a barrier that cannot be overcome—not for that home, anyway.

You will find wildly diverse Cost and Fear issues among your home buyers. Every customer brings his own unique set of wants, needs, and stumbling blocks.

Getting to know your customer on a deep level during your discovery will put you on the path to begin determining his costs and fears.

SOLVING THE FORMULA

Throughout the sales process, the customer constantly reprioritizes these three elements, giving one (or more) of them greater weight and consideration at any given time.

The Buying Formula shows us the relationship and interplay of these elements to each other such that we see people buy when:

Current Dissatisfaction × Future Promise > Cost + Fear

Think about the buying factors for any prospect you've ever worked with, and then place those influencing factors on a scale according to the elements of the Buying Formula.

You can also think back to the last car you purchased and you will see the weighting process that went into that decision. Invariably you will find a combination of all these factors.

The Buying Formula explains why people buy and why they don't buy. On a subconscious level, every one of your customers filters his decision through the Buying Formula.

For those who purchase, the Buying Formula is weighted just enough to the left side of the equation (Current Dissatisfaction × Future Promise). Those who do not purchase get over-weighted on the right side of the equation (Cost + Fear).

A BUYING FORMULA CASE STUDY

Picture yourself spotting your favorite coffee shop at the end of one of "those" days. Your brain says, "This has been a ridiculously rough day (Current Dissatisfaction) and a latte would taste so good! It would make this whole stupid day better! (Future Promise) Yes, four dollars is a lot (Cost), but I deserve it."

Think back to the case study from the salesperson that I overheard in Austin: A family of five in need of a single-story home due to their son's physical and mental challenges.

How high was their Current Dissatisfaction? A "10," correct? They were not staying in their current home. Period.

Let's assume that their Cost and Fear issues could be reasonably accommodated (in other words, they could truly afford to buy the new home). If the salesperson I talked with showed them a Future Promise that was also a "10"—a home that provided everything they were looking for—they would have been in a perfect buying position. It would have been a win/win for everyone!

As salespeople, our goal is to weight the equation on the left side for our customers. You will never (NEVER!) fully eliminate Cost and Fear. Your aim is to provide a solution which clearly outweighs all inhibiting factors *enough*, thus making a purchase decision the only logical choice.

CREATE YOUR OWN CASE STUDY

Think back to the last three homes you sold. Then use the table below to map out the Buying Formula for each of your home buyers:

Customer	Current Dissatisfaction	Future Promise	Cost + Fear

What jumps out at you about your case study customers? Does his purchase decision make total sense to you based on the Buying Formula?

Of course, you know all of this in hindsight now. The key is to strategically discover this information early in the process to enable you in the experiential selling process.

FEEDBACK FROM THE FIELD

Working with sales professionals across the country, I see a pattern when it comes to uncovering Current Dissatisfaction and Future Promise. Consider the following dialogue and see if you can identify the pattern:

> SP: "So, what isn't working for you in your current home?"
>
> B: "Well, we really need a bigger master bathroom."
>
> SP: "Anything else?"
>
> B: "We'd really like a more open kitchen."
>
> SP: "Got it!"

Do you see the pattern? The original question is a Current Dissatisfaction question, but the customer didn't talk about her Current Dissatisfaction. She described her Future Promise. This happens all the time!

Although it helpful to know the customer wants a bigger bathroom and a more open kitchen, it is vital to understand what she is moving from. In other words, what is wrong with her current bathroom and kitchen?

Compare the following dialogue with the dialogue above:

> SP: "So, what isn't working for you in your current home?"
>
> B: "Well, we really need a bigger master bathroom."
>
> SP: "Okay, tell me why your current bathroom feels too small?"

B: "It's just cramped. There is only one sink and my husband and I can barely fit in there at the same time. I usually have to use the hallway bathroom to get ready in the morning and it's just not working!"

SP: "Got it. Anything else not working for you?"

B: "We'd really like a more open kitchen."

SP: "I understand that! Can you tell me about your current kitchen—how does it feel when you're in there?"

Note that in each answer the customer attempted to jump into a description of their Future Promise. Great salespeople know that understanding the *entire* formula is essential in order to weight the equation to the left side. Practice bringing customers back to their Current Dissatisfaction when you are in the discovery process. Doing so will dramatically enhance your ability to create an amazing and memorable experience.

EXPERIENTIAL SELLING ENHANCES FUTURE PROMISE

Experiential selling is all about beefing up the customer's Future Promise. It is about moving beyond a "demonstration" and painting a richly woven experience with your customer that depicts how wonderful his life will be when he moves into his new home.

You see, when Current Dissatisfaction is sky high, and when Future Promise *also* becomes sky high, it is *far* easier to overcome the Cost and Fear issues you might face!

A WORD OF WARNING ABOUT COST + FEAR

Don't try to solve Cost and Fear issues too soon in the process. Yes, gain an understanding of what they may be, but resist the urge to conquer them early on.

You will find that when both Current Dissatisfaction and Future Promise are maximized, Cost and Fear issues start to decrease and your customer becomes far more willing to work through possible solutions in a cooperative and open-minded manner. Therefore, you need time to discover their Current Dissatisfaction and help them experience their Future Promise before you start to tackle Cost and Fear.

When Current Dissatisfaction and Future Promise are clearly defined, customers feel motivated to work with you on Cost and Fear solutions instead of feeling debilitated by them.

> "The oldest and strongest emotion of mankind is fear, and the oldest and strongest kind of fear is fear of the unknown."
>
> *H.P. Lovecraft*

As we move into the technique portion of this book, let me encourage you to keep the Buying Formula at the front of your mind. (Write it down on your bookmark if that helps!) Every technique explained in the following pages is built on the foundation of the Buying Formula.

Current Dissatisfaction (CD)
x Future Promise (FP) > Cost + Fear (CF)

USING THE BUYING FORMULA FOR FOLLOW-UP

The Buying Formula is a great tool when following up with a prospect. Follow-up can be difficult for salespeople because we often don't know what to say when we make that call.

We end up saying something lame like, *"Hey, it's Amy. Just following up. Have you made any decisions yet? Oh, you haven't. Okay. Well, let me know. Bye-eee!"*

If you use the Buying Formula as your guide (revisiting the buyer's CD and FP) your follow-up messages will be personal and relevant: *"Hey, it's Amy. I was just thinking about you on my drive home. I know you are probably putting your kids to bed right now and I know that having the twins share a room has become a real frustration. As I recall, you described the nightly battles as 'maddening' and 'exhausting.' I want to let you know I am thinking of you and I believe that four-bedroom we looked at would bring some much needed peace to your world! Give me a call. Let's talk about it."*

APPLICATION QUESTIONS

Ask yourself these questions as you plan to use the Buying Formula as your sales guide.

1. How can I get to a deeper level of understanding regarding my customer's Current Dissatisfaction? What are the questions I should ask and how should I phrase them?

2. How do I better understand what a customer desires by way of Future Promise? How can I discover these "hot buttons" early in the conversation?

3. How do I feel about my progress thus far in the process of reconstructing my sales presentation in order to maximize the customer's experience?

Now take a moment to write a commitment to yourself. What will you do with what you have just learned?

. . . .

. . . .

. . . .

. . . .

. . . .

. . . .

. . . .

. . . .

. . . .

. . . .

. . . .

SECTION THREE –

Experiential Selling Strategies

CHAPTER 9:

. . . .

Transitioning from the Discovery to the Experience

WHEN TO MAKE THE TRANSITION

By now you should feel fully pre-pared to lead your customers through a unique and highly per-sonalized experience as an extension of your deep and thorough discov-ery of their Current Dissatisfaction and Future Promise.

> "Enthusiasm is excitement with inspiration, motivation, and a pinch of creativity."
> *Bo Bennett*

But how do you know *when* to cut off that initial discovery and begin to lead your customers through an experience of their new lives?

The answer lies in these two simple but powerful questions you should ask yourself:

1. Do I know enough about this customer to truly create a one-of-a-kind experience of the home I am about to show him?

2. Will I be able to construct a compelling Future Promise that will serve to amplify his Current Dissatisfaction?

Your response to these questions serves as the answer for whether it is time for you to move on or not.

If your discovery is too short, you will find that you do not know how to stage an experience that resonates with the customer's specific situation, and thus you will lose the opportunity to create an emotional connection for them. But if your discovery goes on too long, you risk frustrating your customer by spending time on cumbersome details.

Here is another mental benchmark to determine if it is time to begin sharing the home. Reset your thinking so that the goal of your initial discovery is NOT to get the customer excited about seeing a home.

Your goal is to get to know the customer so well that YOU feel excited about showing him a home!

Make sense?

FOCUS YOUR DISCOVERY QUESTIONS

Don't ask anything in your original discovery that you cannot immediately utilize in the experience of the home. Questions about financing, terms, market conditions, etc. all take up time and mental energy, but are not really relevant at this point.

I like to say that in discovery, you are not selling anything and you are not solving anything. Discovery is all about listening to the buyer. Of course, if your customer brings these topics up, you must address them, but do so only briefly and with a promise to get back to them later. The more topics you talk about before she sees a home, the harder it is for her to see what you show her with fresh eyes and a clear mind. (Beware of buyer brain overload!)

HOW TO MAKE THE TRANSITION

When you know the time is right, the next step is to graciously define your role as the leader of the experience ahead.

There is absolutely zero reason to ask for permission to lead the customer in this process. YOU are the professional. YOU are the expert. YOU are the "assistant buyer." You can and must fulfill your duty in leading the way.

DON'T ASK FOR PERMISSION TO DO YOUR JOB

Commit right now to striking this sentence from your vocabulary: "Would you like me to walk through the home with you?" In fact, take a pen and draw a line through that sentence right now. Let's eradicate this damaging phrase from the real estate sales lexicon here and now, shall we?

As the sales professional, you want to lead your prospect into a positive emotional zone. Here's how.

SETTING THE EMOTIONAL STAGE

Imagine you are tasked with setting up two friends for a blind date. You think they'll be a great match and will get along famously. You want this to happen.

Here is what you are likely NOT to say as you introduce this idea to one of your two friends:

> *"He's 5-10, 180 pounds, in generally good shape, sees his dentist on a regular basis, is mild in nature, good breeding material, has blood type O-positive, and he likes to do Sudoku puzzles."*

Gee, how could your friend *possibly* resist such a compelling and charming description as that?! This description does not, in any way, convey the fact that you really truly want this match to happen.

You are much more likely to say something like this:

> *"Tommy is a great guy! He's funny, interesting, and a really good conversationalist. He makes everyone around him feel comfortable. He calls his mom every week (I know, right?!), loves kids, and even though he is an athlete he's not a "dumb jock"…the guy reads Shakespeare for crying out loud! Oh, and did I mention that he looks like a male model?!"*

That would be more like it, yes?

I mean, how ridiculous is it to describe what should be an emotional experience in dry, analytical terms? Not only is it ridiculous and not compelling, it could even be off-putting!

And yet that is what happens in home sales every single day.

It is up to you to create a strong and positive emotional tone for buyers. You are setting them up on a blind (ish) date and you want this to happen!

Give yourself and your customer permission to enjoy the process as the real, live human beings that you are!

CREATING A POSITIVE EMOTIONAL SPARK

Set up the experience with a brief and emotionally engaged overview of the home you are about to show. Just one or two sentences are all you need.

> "Flaming enthusiasm, backed up by horse sense and persistence, is the quality that most frequently makes for success."
> *Dale Carnegie*

You want two achieve two primary objectives:

1) Transfer positive energy to your customer
2) Explain why you feel so excited for your customer to see this particular home

This approach allows you to impact the customer's attitude *before* he walks through the door. You want to lead him into a positive mindset in which he is anticipating that something good is about to happen.

Think of a restaurant server describing the special of the day. We hear this description in two possible ways:

Version One:

> *"It looks good. A lot of people are ordering it. It's not my favorite dish, no matter how it's prepared, so I'm probably the wrong person to ask."*

Version Two:

> *"Oh my word, it's amazing! I had it for dinner earlier this evening and it's one of the best dishes I've had since I started working here. You have to get it!"*

If you decide to order the special based on version two, you will do so with great anticipation. Similarly, your home buying customer takes her emotional cue from you. If you exude genuine excitement about "the special," your customer will feel excited, too!

Your introduction might sound something like this:

> *"I'm really excited to show you this home because it represents so much of the life you want to live. I don't want you to just tour the home; I want you to try it on for size. Mentally move in and we'll see if it's a good fit. Let's go!"*

FOUR COMPONENTS OF AN ENGAGING TRANSITION

Let's break this down in a little more detail. Here are the four components of a strong, emotionally engaged home introduction:

1. Be excited in your delivery—enthusiasm is contagious.

2. Make it about the buyer. When possible, refer back to things you learned in discovery.

3. Use elegant and inspiring language that grabs attention. (i.e., don't be boring!)

4. Make it actionable at the end.

I encourage you to practice your introductions on the next few homes you plan to show *before* you try this with a customer. Practicing with a peer will make your practice time even more productive!

PRACTICING YOUR TRANSITION

Take a minute and think about a home you are currently selling and let's practice scripting out a powerful home introduction.

Let me give you a customer profile:

> *Dan and Barbara both received promotions in the past year, so they feel that their lives are really on an upswing. They live in an older, smaller "starter" home with small rooms and a small backyard. They are not thrilled with the school their two young children will be attending in their current neighborhood. They want a home in a neighborhood that reflects their career success and that provides larger rooms and more open space for their family.*

Now, in the space below, write out a customized transition statement full of positive energy and emotion:

· ·

· ·

· ·

· ·

· ·

· ·

· ·

· ·

· ·

· ·

· ·

APPLICATION QUESTIONS

Think about these questions as you consider your own opportunities for growth:

1. Reflect back on your last several presentations. Did you know your customers well enough to create emotion-based experiences?

2. Do you sometimes get stuck in conversations that only serve to muddy up the process? What can you do/say to diminish and defer those conversations?

3. Do you have a strategic lead-up to the experience? Is it based on emotion or is it more technical and analytical?

Take a few moments to write a commitment to creating a new approach to how you introduce the homes you show:

CHAPTER 10:

Leveraging Emotional Altitude

> Emotional altitude is a measure of a buyer's positive emotional engagement with a home.

THE TRANSFERENCE OF POSITIVE ENERGY

Have you ever walked into a store or restaurant and been greeted by someone who was so incredibly positive that it was contagious? I'm not talking about the obnoxious person with phony, over-the-top giddiness. I'm referring to someone with genuine enthusiasm who makes you want to adopt the same kind of positivity for yourself.

When you walk through Disneyland, you see this kind of energy on the faces of the "cast members" throughout the park. Disneyland is a positive energy place and the people there reflect that ideal.

This same vibe is present at certain coffee shops and restaurants. If you live in the Western United States like I do, you probably know that Dutch Bros. Coffee and In-n-Out Burger are

> "Enthusiasm is the mother of effort, and without it nothing great was ever achieved."
> *Ralph Waldo Emerson*

great examples of businesses where the employees are wholly committed to being positive and enthusiastic. (If you have never experienced the Dutch Bros. level of positivity, I encourage you to seek out one of these drive-through coffee shops ASAP. If you think caffeine wakes you up, just wait until you meet a Dutch Bros. employee!)

This is precisely what we need a whole lot more of in the sales presentation, especially as it relates to the showing of a home. The sales professional plays a huge role in monitoring and even altering the customer's energy level.

This is about far more than setting the emotional tone. There is an important psychological factor at play, a concept that few people (buyers or sellers) are actively aware of. I call it *emotional endorsement.*

Here's the long and short of emotional endorsement: If they like you, and you like the product, then *they* will like the product. You offer emotional endorsement with your heart, not your head. Your customers adopt the energy and enthusiasm you have about the homes you show. It's how human beings work: We are highly susceptible to genuine enthusiasm—our psychological immune systems just can't fight it off!

If you think about it, emotional endorsement really is the basis for *all* referrals, whether it is your friends telling you what movie you should go see, your financial advisor telling you what stock you should invest in, or a trusted salesperson telling a buyer what home is best for him. It's how we function. And when we know enough about each other to make relevant recommendations, it works!

CAPITALIZING ON A BUYER'S EMOTIONAL ALTITUDE

The process of shopping for a home invariably takes a customer through a variety of emotions. Sometimes those emotions are positive and sometimes they are negative. We want to enhance the customer's experience by elevating the positive emotion—by increasing what we call *emotional altitude.*

> "The business of the poet is not to find new emotions, but to use the ordinary ones and, in working them up into poetry, to express feelings which are not in actual emotions at all."
> *T. S. Eliot*

Emotional altitude is a measure of a buyer's positive emotional engagement with a home. Emotional altitude escalates when we help a home buyer envision the positive future experience of living in a particular home. This altitude is sustained as a customer continually thinks in a positive manner.

One way to maximize emotional altitude is to ask the customer questions about her life rather than just point out features in the home. If you do your job right during the discovery, you should be able to help the customer mentally move in.

> Example: If a husband and wife were joking (but were also serious) about her need for an extra large closet with plenty of shoe storage space during the discovery, you might say something like, *"In all seriousness, does this closet look like it will be sufficient for your fabulous shoe collection?"*

Think back to The 4:2 Formula conversation you had with your customer and draw on that information to ask specific questions about a hobby, family tradition, a favorite piece of furniture, etc. Direct your customer's focus to the emotional realities of her life and lead her in bringing those points forward.

WOULD YOU BUY FROM YOU?

The burden of sustaining emotional altitude rests on the shoulders of the sales professional. You are charged with protecting the energy and sustaining the positive vibe in the sales process.

A quick test of where your energy needs to be at is to simply ask yourself: "Would I want my customer to adopt the energy level I have right now?"

Another way to put that: "Do I have enough positive energy for myself *and* my customer?"

To be clear, this does not mean you need to be some sort of frantic, over-the-top, hyperactive freak. You don't want to come off like a Jack Russell Terrier who got into a case of Red Bull. But you do need to radiate positive energy and you need to sustain that throughout the process.

> "When you discover your mission, you will feel its demand. It will fill you with enthusiasm and a burning desire to get to work on it."
> *W. Clement Stone*

Your customer will take his emotional cue from you. Give him the opportunity to become emotionally engaged in the experience of viewing a home.

APPLICATION QUESTIONS

Take some time to reflect on the following questions. They will help you determine how you can best manage emotional altitude for yourself and your customers.

1. What holds you back? Do you struggle with appropriately showing your own emotion?

2. Do you find yourself in emotional troughs at certain points during your presentation? What can you do to correct that?

3. How can you sustain a positive emotional altitude throughout the sales experience?

Now take a few moments to write a very concrete definition of what you WILL do to sustain emotional altitude.

. . . .

. . . .

. . . .

. . . .

. . . .

. . . .

. . . .

. . . .

. . . .

. . . .

. . . .

. . . .

. . . .

CHAPTER 11:

Six Simple Experiential Selling Strategies

A number of considerations are in play as you think through the strategy of experiential selling. Consider the following strategic options.

STRATEGY #1: DIALOGUE VS. MONOLOGUE

I stated earlier that most salespeople simply talk too much during a home showing. And the root cause of feature dumping always flows from the same source: Salespeople feature dump because they don't know their customers well enough. It's a fill-in-the-silence technique. Ugh.

The best sales presentation follows a 50/50 pattern. The salesperson talks about fifty percent of the time. You cannot do this when you are feature dumping. The only way to accomplish the 50/50 pattern is to ask a lot of questions.

> You can achieve a more balanced presentation by allowing the customer to find the value.

Too many salespeople believe they should operate as the primary identifier of value. Think about that for a moment. What are the ramifications of this belief?

If I point out high ceilings, I am sharing a feature. If my customers point out high ceilings, they are building value and it creates a powerful step toward acceptance and closing. People don't argue with themselves, nor do they think themselves dumb or annoying for pointing out something obvious.

When customers identify value, they are selling themselves and they feel thankful that you, the salesperson, allowed them the opportunity to find what they want and need. When you point out value, they feel like you are trying to talk them into something.

> "Price is what you pay. Value is what you get."
> *Warren Buffett*

Let customers identify their own value points. When they do, it makes the closing process much, much easier.

This principle also holds true in regard to objections. Don't fear the customer objection—you *want* your customers talking about their concerns. This is an important part of the dialogue.

That said, here is a common question we get in sales training: "What if they don't like it?" Newsflash: If they don't like it, they don't like it. What matters is whether or not you *know* they don't like it! Ignorance, in this case, is most definitely not bliss.

STRATEGY #2: MACRO VS. MICRO

Think about home shopping from the buyer's perspective. Is it easier to ascertain value from the bottom up or from the top down?

Is it easier to make a value judgment by assembling all the details about a home and then making one major decision, or is it more simple to decide on the top level if you like something and then justify your choice with the details?

Customers look for cognitive ease in the buying process. They take mental shortcuts in order to keep everything straight in their minds. One way to help them do this is to think "Macro to Micro" in your presentation. Gain agreement on the big stuff *first* and then go back to the details.

> "Coming to understand a painting or a symphony in an unfamiliar style, to recognize the work of an artist or school, to see or hear in new ways, is as cognitive an achievement as learning to read or write or add."
> *Nelson Goodman*

Showing homes in a micro-first style is like trying to evaluate an art master-piece by starting with an explanation of the smallest brush strokes. You must begin by looking at the big picture if you want to get full emotional engagement.

This is true for all aspects of the home buying decision. The details are important, but they only make sense in context. Later in this book, we will examine the details of the macro-to-micro approach. (See what I did there?)

HOME EXPERIENCE VS. MUSEUM TOUR

We of course want to respect the homes we show our buyers. But, it is important to remember that great experiences feel more like a test drive than a museum tour.

Often, when I see salespeople walking a buyer through a home, it's almost as if there are imaginary red velvet ropes blocking off entry into each room. Both the salespeople and the buyers look like they are being careful to not cross into any forbidden spaces such as the perfectly staged family room.

The unspoken message is: *Do not touch! Stay out!* This is insane. You are showing people *homes*. What do you do in *your* home? I'm guessing you sit on the furniture and actually touch things!

To provide a full and accurate experience, give your buyers the time, freedom, and encouragement to *really* experience the spaces in a home. Help them get a sense of what it would really feel like to live there. Any time you are about to say to a buyer, "Can you picture yourself...?" instead ask yourself, "Can I actually have them do it?"

STRATEGY #3: STAR VS. FACILITATOR

Who is the star here? Too many salespeople act like the home showing is their moment to shine, sort of a "lights, camera, action" approach. I believe the salesperson actually ranks third in the order of importance.

In the experiential selling process, the customer must remain the number one star. The number two star becomes the home itself. Then comes the salesperson.

In essence, the salesperson plays the role of facilitator in the most literal sense of the word. You facilitate an understanding of a life experience for your customer in a new home. You connect your customers to their new lives. Be proud of your role. You are changing their world!

> "Do you wish to rise? Begin by descending. You plan a tower that will pierce the clouds? Lay first the foundation of humility."
> *Saint Augustine*

STRATEGY #4: THIS VS. THAT (HELPING CUSTOMERS NARROW TO ONE)

Purchasing a home can quickly turn into a mind-numbing experience. It's a far cry from shopping for something like toothpaste, where all of the product choices are fairly similar and the consequences of choosing one you aren't happy with are minimal.

When buying a home, a customer is on the hunt for the best possible option out of myriad choices and if she makes a "wrong" or "bad" choice, she feels like the consequences will be monumental.

This creates a problem because an abundance of choice leads to cognitive strain in the customer's mind. That strain, if left unchecked, raises her stress level.

The brain's default reaction in times of stress is to hit the abort button. The brain will suggest (very convincingly) that it's just not worth it and the customer goes back to what she knows best—the home she lives in now. The pain of dissatisfaction can be cognitively one-upped by the pain of change. (Dang it!)

> "The greatest weapon against stress is our ability to choose one thought over another."
> *William James*

So, how do you simplify the narrowing process in order to protect your customer from defaulting to that which she knows but which isn't best for her? How do you protect her from herself? How exactly can you be a psychological sales superhero? I'll tell you.

THREE TIPS FOR NARROWING CHOICES

1) **Limit the number of active choices at any given time.** It is never in the best interest of your customer to have more than a couple of choices in mind. Encourage her to actively eliminate the homes that are not at the top of her list.

2) **Get her comfortable with compromise.** Too many times we see home buyers struggle because of things that wouldn't be their first choice. They need to understand and accept that compromise is a natural part of the process.

3) **Teach her that the goal is "best," not "perfect."** If your customer is looking for "the perfect home," she is going to end up disappointed. It doesn't exist. Teach her that she is looking for the *best* available home for her family—nothing more and nothing less.

STRATEGY #5: SYMBOLIC SELLING

If you are a Realtor®, you'll typically get paid on just about anything your client purchases. But if you are working for a builder in new home sales, you are competing with myriad other buyer options. How do you make your homes stand out?

DON'T DARE TO COMPARE

We recommend that our clients stay away from the "dare to compare" worksheets that are so common today. This "tool" directs a prospect to look at a long list of features and compare which builders include all of those items in their homes.

Not only is this an incredibly tedious task for the customer, it also assumes (erroneously) that all value is created equal. Yes, you may offer something that the competitor does not, but if that feature is of no value to a specific customer, you are wasting your time having him make a comparison.

We teach our clients a technique called symbolic selling. The goal with this technique is to focus on a few value differentiators—things you have that your key competitor does not offer—and describe those elements in a way that helps your customer understand that they would be seriously compromising if they bought anything else.

For example, suppose you offer tray ceilings as a standard item, and your competitor doesn't offer them at all. You can say to your customer, "You said you are living in an apartment right now. Many builders only offer flat ceilings that look exactly like your apartment, but our homes have these very tall tray ceilings. You see these in million dollar homes! This is one of the ways you know you are getting a quality built home."

With this statement, you are trying to get the customer to see that buying from a competitor isn't really an option at all. To do so would be to purchase a home that is too similar to their current residence and thus, unacceptable.

> "Why fit in when you were born to stand out?"
> *Dr. Seuss*

Here is the key to making symbolic selling work for you. Whatever feature you are talking about has to mean something to your customer. (For example, tray ceilings are relevant to someone who lives in an apartment). Remember the experiential selling rule: customer first, home second.

Let's say this customer leaves your sales office and heads right over to your competition. What do you think he will look for in the model?

That's right! Tray ceilings. When your competitors do not offer them, your customer will not only think he is settling for less by purchasing a home from them, but your home will actually be at the front of his mind...while talking to your competitor!

STRATEGY #6: HERE VS. THERE (UNDERSTANDING WHERE TO START)

When you walk into a home with a customer, where do you go first? If you are like most salespeople, you begin in the entryway. That seems to make sense. Then the living area, then the kitchen, etc.

Question: Is this approach strategic or reactive? Are you walking through the spaces in a home in this order simply because that's what is in front of you? What if you intentionally designed the sequence of a home tour based on the customer's wants and needs? (Once again: customer first, house second.)

> Remember the most important strategy in experiential selling: customer first, home second.

I believe the best place to begin a home tour is wherever you find the strongest convergence of the customer's hot buttons and what a home has to offer. This is the difference between merely showing a home as it comes and customizing the experience for an individual home buyer. It's a *huge* difference!

Suppose you are selling a home to someone who is coming from a very dated house with a horrible kitchen. The kitchen is her hot button and her current pain is substantial. She hates her kitchen and is embarrassed to have friends over. Let's further suppose that the entry and living areas in the home you are selling are not all that special or they don't really mean much to your customer.

> "The essence of strategy is choosing what not to do."
> *Michael Porter*

What happens to the emotional altitude if you start in the entryway? If you have done your job well, before she walks through the front door, her emotional altitude is high because she is anticipating something great.

As you pause in the entryway and living areas, her emotional altitude dips— it is just not that exciting to her. Now you must ramp her energy level back up for the tour of the kitchen because your choice to begin in the entryway actually *deflated* her emotional altitude.

The solution is simple: Do the tour differently. Move through the entryway quickly and walk the customer straight into the beautiful kitchen. Now what happens to her emotional altitude?

The strong emotions of anticipation that she felt before she entered the house carry through into the kitchen experience. Now the emotional altitude is sky high as she falls in love with this beautiful, magazine-quality chef's kitchen! How do you suppose she is going to feel now about the rest of home—even the unimportant areas like the entryway?

In some cases, you might even want to start in the back yard. When I was in the market for a home last year, if the yard didn't work, the deal was over. That's where we started the tour—out back. I loved the yard of the house we ended up buying so much that I was willing to overlook deficiencies inside the home.

Remember the most important strategy in experiential selling: ***customer first, home second.*** Let the unique traits and desires of each customer's situation dictate the sequence of how you show a home.

CONNECTING THE EXPERIENCE TO REAL LIFE

Several days after I taught an Experiential Selling seminar in southern California, I received a call from one of the attendees in the class. He shared with me how he was able to create an amazing experience for some recent customers of his.

He was working with a family who was looking for more space. After digging a little deeper to gain clarity, he discovered that their current kitchen was driving the wife crazy. In their home, the dad often wrestles with their two hyperactive boys in the only living space they have. Guess where that space is? Right next to the kitchen!

When the salesperson learned this, he realized that he needed to show this family how wrestling could still happen, while giving Mom her sanity back. Here's how he did it.

He took the mom to the kitchen and asked her to stay there and get a feel for the space. He then took the dad and kids to the bonus room. Rather than saying, "Can you imagine wrestling here with your kids?" this salesperson moved the coffee table out of the way and asked the kids and their dad to try out the new wrestling ring! The dad looked at him as if to say, "Are you serious?" Of course, he was. So sure enough, they started wrestling.

The salesperson then ran downstairs to the mom and said, "Well, the kids are wrestling with Dad. How does this compare to your current home?" With that, the mom was sold on the kitchen space and her newfound peace of mind.

APPLICATION QUESTIONS

Consider these questions as you evaluate your own presentation:

1. Am I guilty of talking too much during the sales presentation? Should I be dramatically increasing the number of questions I ask?

2. Is the experience I am creating too much about me and not enough about my customer and the home? How can I draw the focus back to the customer and then to the home?

3. Am I confusing my customers with too many choices? How can I more quickly narrow their search down to one home? (Hint: Start with your discovery questions!)

4. Am I strategic in the way I walk someone through a home? Am I setting up the tour according to each customer's unique wants and needs?

Now write down your thoughts on how to make some immediate improvements to your overall strategy, based on what you just learned.

. . . .

. . . .

. . . .

. . . .

. . . .

. . . .

. . . .

. . . .

. . . .

. . . .

. . . .

CHAPTER 12:

Moving From Macro to Micro

In Chapter Eleven I mentioned the strategic concept of selling from "Macro to Micro." This means getting the customer to agree to big-picture value before moving into a description of specific features and details.

Using the Macro to Micro strategy, experiential selling begins with how the customer becomes familiar with (in order):

- Region/City
- Neighborhood/Community
- Street Scene
- Exterior and Front Yard
- Entry to the Home
- Each Individual Room
- Specific Features

Notice how this list moves from a macro view to a micro view. Let's begin by establishing a sense of place for our customer.

REGION/CITY

Every human wants to experience a sense of place. It is part of our core makeup—it is intrinsic and universal.

Place recognition begins with the region or city in which we live and that we identify with. People identify themselves as living in the San Francisco Bay Area, Chicagoland, or Greater Toronto, even though their actual address is more specific than that.

The adage "location, location, location" begins with a specific sense of place in the world. Local identity is made up of sports teams, regional festivals, fashion, food choices, weather, and cultural quirks.

> "A sense of place results gradually and unconsciously from inhabiting a landscape over time, becoming familiar with its physical properties, accruing history within its confines."
> *Kent Rydon*

Establishing a sense of place is especially important for buyers who are relocating and do not yet identify with the culture of their new surrounds. Often, relocation buyers are going through the buying process against their own desires. They are following their job, but perhaps they would have rather stayed where they were.

In these cases, the salesperson is no longer representing only a home or a company. She is now an ambassador for an entire region. You are doing a great service to your relocation buyers when you help them understand the unique nuances of their new environs.

Become an expert in how to share the value of your region or city. This includes understanding local culture, commute distances, climate trends, economics, political leanings, and more.

AMY'S PRO TIP:

A great tool to use when learning about a region/city and neighborhood/community (and more) is TweetDeck. This social media application provides a quick and easy way to search Twitter for key words or phrases to find trending articles on the topics you are most interested in. TweetDeck is a must-have for all savvy salespeople!

NEIGHBORHOOD/COMMUNITY

Customers want and need to connect to a more intimate sense of place within a region or city. While they use macro terms ("We moved to the Pacific Northwest") to tell people from other parts of the country where they live, their day-to-day living has everything to do with a specific neighborhood. A person may *move* to New York City, but he *lives* in Murray Hill or Jackson Heights.

A community is defined not by borders but by amenities. Think of where you reside today. My guess is that you define your community in terms of:

- Living style (urban, rural, etc.)
- Shopping
- Dining
- Schools
- Traffic patterns
- Recreation
- Churches

My address is in Newcastle, California, but my community encompasses Auburn, Loomis, Rocklin, and Roseville.

The savvy salesperson will quickly discover the nuances of each community in which she sells. This equips her to be in the position of "know everything; share what matters." This is critical because many buyers shop in multiple communities.

When my wife and I were shopping for a home, we ended up looking in no less than five different areas covering more than fifty square miles. Each area presented us with slightly different day-to-day realities.

RYAN'S PRO TIP:

Talk with the locals, especially local business owners. They can tell you the ins and outs of micro-communities and can fill you in on unique value points. Get out there— do some shopping, go sit and enjoy a cup of coffee, talk to people. The more you learn and personally experience about this area, the stronger your emotional endorsement will become.

STREET SCENE

Are you an exterior buyer or an interior buyer? What about your customers— what are they?

Years ago, Builder Magazine and Eliant teamed up for a massive survey of new home buyers. One interesting piece of information from that survey stood out to me: Two-thirds of home buyers are most interested in a home's floorplan; one-third are most interested in a home's exterior and street scene.

That's a startling statistic, because it exposes a consistent flaw in the home selling process. Far too many salespeople begin their presentation only after they walk through the front door. This leaves one-third of buyers on their own to figure out whether the location and street scene are working for them.

> "The key is falling in love with something, anything. If your heart's attached to it, then your mind will be attached to it."
> *Vera Wang*

Even interior buyers desire a sense of place. They want to feel comfortable in their neighborhood and on their street. The surrounding street scene is a critical but typically overlooked element in establishing value.

A neighborhood *must* resonate with your customer. It is your job to get him to pay attention so he can hear and see what a neighborhood has to offer. Do this by asking your customer to intentionally observe and absorb the surroundings.

THREE STEPS FOR CREATING A STREET SCENE EXPERIENCE

1) **Find a street scene moment.** On your way to the home, you want your customer to see other residents enjoying the neighborhood. If you see someone washing her car, getting her mail, or walking her dog, stop there. (Dog-walking is always the best option if it's available.) You are not trying to be tricky here—you are simply trying to place the customer in what real life will be on this street.

2) **Stop your car across the street.** Park across from and slightly up or slightly down from the home you are about to show. Ultimately, you want to be within sight of the home but not so close that the customer's attention is drawn to the home just yet. This is a very brief stop, allowing you to perform a quick "street scene close."

3) **Ask a "feel close" question.** This is not heavy duty at all. The question should be very comfortable and conversational. For example: *"I just wanted to give you a quick look at the street before we get to the house. Do you like what you're seeing here?"*

APPLICATION QUESTIONS

Some questions to ask yourself about your approach:

1. Do I fully understand and embrace my role as an ambassador of both my region and specific communities?

2. What can I do to learn more about the location I am selling? Who can I talk with?

3. Do I pay enough attention to the street scene? Would my buyers appreciate it if I did?

Now jot down some ideas and commitments about how to improve in this area. Be specific.

. . . .

. . . .

. . . .

. . . .

. . . .

. . . .

. . . .

. . . .

. . . .

. . . .

. . . .

. . . .

. . . .

SECTION FOUR –

Creating the Experience

CHAPTER 13:

Three Tips for the Exterior Experience

It's Marketing 101: If people like the packaging, they are more inclined to like the product inside of it.

I bet right now you can think of some boxes you would be excited to receive even if you had no idea what was in them. A small robin's egg blue box perhaps? A sleek Apple box? The saying, "Don't judge a book by its cover," exists for a reason: because we do!

Our brains operate in shortcuts. In his book *Blink*, Malcolm Gladwell explores the idea of "thin-slicing," taking small observation points and completing the picture of them in one's mind.

In *Thinking, Fast and Slow*, Dr. Daniel Kahneman explores the idea of heuristics, mental rules of thumb that make it easier to make decisions based on limited exposure to details. Home buyers unconsciously use thin-slicing and heuristics like crazy, and perhaps never more than when it comes to curb appeal.

> How the customers feel about the outside of the home has a powerful bearing on how they feel about the inside of the home.

A slew of psychological factors are at play when it comes to assessing curb appeal. In many ways, curb appeal is not unlike evaluating art. I might not be able to tell you *why* I love or hate a painting right off the bat, but nonetheless, my convictions are strong.

When selecting a home, how the customers feel about the outside has a powerful bearing on how they feel about the inside. Your customers' love of an exterior plants a seed of desire in them to love the interior.

Of course this does not mean that loving a home's interior is guaranteed, only that the inclination to fall in love is greatly increased when exterior love is pre-established. It's like driving past a great-*looking* restaurant you have never been to and saying, "I bet *that* place has good food!" You get the idea.

We want our customers to be in a pleasant frame of mind when they go inside the home we show them. We accomplish this by first creating a compelling exterior experience.

BUT WHAT IF THEY HATE THE EXTERIOR?

You might be asking, "Don't I run the risk of raising an objection if I ask them for their opinion up front?"

Well, let's start with some blunt truth. If they hate it, they hate it. The real question is whether or not you know about their displeasure.

As previously stated, ignorance is NOT bliss when it comes to knowing what your customer likes and what they do not like.

You must determine *why* they don't like it and then discover whether their dislike is a deal-killer or not.

THREE TIPS FOR THE EXTERIOR EXPERIENCE

1. **Begin at a Distance**

   How: Park across the street. A home is best viewed from a bit of a distance. This is largely due to being able to see the home in perspective, relative to the homes on either side. Another plus: When you are evaluating a home's exterior from across the street, the overall home site looks bigger and the home itself does not tower over you. How a home orients on the site is also clear from across the street.

Why: Viewing a home is·all about perspective and sightlines. If you stand too close to the front of a home, you can't see the space between it and the houses next door. If you stand across the street, you see the gaps, making the site appear larger.

2. **Keep it General**

How: Don't share too much detail. You may be a construction and architecture expert, but most of your customers are not. It's easy to confuse or lose people with too many details. That said, be prepared to describe the exterior of a home in a simple but elegant way.

> "Simplicity is the glory of expression."
> *Walt Whitman*

Why: If any details are going to be shared, your customers should be the ones sharing them. If they like the exterior, ask them what they specifically find attractive. By simply stating what they like, they are increasing their positive emotions toward the home.

ONE OF MY BIGGEST PET PEEVES

Using the word "elevation" instead of "exterior" with buyers.

My first job out of graduate school was with a private builder in Atlanta, Georgia, and I was as green as they come. I knew nothing about homebuilding but wanted to impress my new coworkers and managers.

The topography in Atlanta is uneven so the homes sit at varying heights on the homesites. For the longest time, everyone kept talking about "elevation" and I just assumed they meant how high a home sat above the road.

Remember to keep "real estate speak" out of the experience.

3. **Close on the Exterior**

> **How:** Take the opportunity for a calm, conversational close here. Keep it very simple, something along the lines of: "Do you like the look of this home"? It doesn't have to be anything more than that, but you do want to make sure you ask the question.
>
> **Why:** If they love it, you have influenced the way they will perceive the interior. If they hate it, well…you kinda want to know that!

Notice that the technique for creating an exterior experience does not take very long, nor should it. This is simply a matter of gaining acceptance and agreement before entering the home.

In doing so, you put your customer into a positive and anticipatory state when she walks through the front door—raising emotional altitude and moving yourself one step closer to the sale.

GAINING AGREEMENTS ALONG THE WAY

Too many people selling new homes wait until they get to the contract to ask buyers which exterior design they prefer. Here's a thought: Instead of waiting until contract, get that decision out of the way while showing the home.

If you are with a customer who doesn't like the exterior design of your model, you might address the design options and casually ask, *"Out of these five design options, which one feels like the right one for you?"*

Or you might say, *"If you had to pick one design, which one would it be?"* That, my friends, is a small buying decision that makes your final close a lot easier on both you and the customer!

APPLICATION QUESTIONS

Consider these questions regarding your own technique:

1. Has the exterior been somewhat of an afterthought in my presentations?

2. How can I increase emotional acceptance of the home and of how the home complements the street scene?

3. What does a simple and conversational closing question sound like for me?

Now take a moment to commit to a new and better technique in this vital area.

. . . .

. . . .

. . . .

. . . .

. . . .

. . . .

. . . .

. . . .

. . . .

. . . .

. . . .

. . . .

. . . .

. . . .

CHAPTER 14:

Creating a Grand Entrance

> Entering the home might be the single most critical moment in the experiential selling process.

Over the past thirty years I have observed, either in person or by watching video mystery shops, more sales presentations than I can count. When it comes to botched technique, nothing stands out more than the way most salespeople walk their customers into a home.

What should be a magical moment for the prospect is almost always treated as a routine, nothing moment by salespeople. If you want to up your game immediately, start here.

Entering the home might be the single most critical moment in the experiential selling process. If your buyers hate the feel of a home upon entry, it's going to be a tough uphill battle. If they love the entry, they will be inclined to like the rest of the home. (Think about every saying you've heard about first impressions: You only get one chance to make them…Your first impression is your last impression…etc.)

More importantly, entrance into the home establishes the emotional altitude for the entire experience. Starting on a flat emotional note will all but guarantee a mediocre presentation throughout.

Here are three common technique fails to watch out for:

GRAND ENTRANCE FAIL #1: ENTERING THE HOME BEFORE YOUR CUSTOMER DOES.

This is such a simple thing but it is a common problem. Salespeople enter the home first about 90% of the time. When doing so, they completely block their customer's view. Simply let your customer enter the home without his primary view being your backside and voilà, you have just made a significant improvement to your presentation! (No offense to your backside. I'm certain it provides a lovely view.)

GRAND ENTRANCE FAIL #2: TALKING THROUGHOUT THE GRAND ENTRANCE.

The entryway wants to say something to the customer. Actually, it wants to sing. Alas, all too often that song cannot be heard because a salesperson is jabbering away throughout the process. Here's an idea: Shut up and let the magic happen.

> "Silence is a source of great strength."
> *Lao Tzu*

GRAND ENTRANCE FAIL #3: NOT PAUSING TO MAKE IT "A MOMENT."

Your customer needs to take it all in. Even just a few seconds of silence can let her absorb what she is seeing. This is the big reveal. Let it be special. Make it a moment.

For the customer, the entry represents a subconscious esoteric evaluation. Many find this moment difficult to define but very powerful nonetheless. This is why I recommend you do not ask for specifics; simply ask your customers how they feel after they have absorbed the setting for a few moments.

Here are five technique tips to help you create a powerfully compelling Grand Entrance:

GRAND ENTRANCE TECHNIQUE #1: PAUSE JUST OUTSIDE THE FRONT DOOR.

This does not need to be some grandiose gesture, but you do want to help your customer focus in on this important opportunity.

GRAND ENTRANCE TECHNIQUE #2: OFFER SOME BRIEF INSTRUCTIONS.

You can give your customer a very simple plan that will maximize the way he sees the home. For example: *"Your impressions when you first walk into the home are critical. I want you to go first, take two steps in, and then tell me how you feel."*

CONTROLLING THE NEXT STEPS

I was always afraid to let customers walk into the home before me. I feared they would take off on me and I would lose control of the presentation. The key to what Jeff is teaching here is in the instructions: *"Take two steps in and then tell me how you feel."* Notice how the wording is very specific.

GRAND ENTRANCE TECHNIQUE #3: LET THE CUSTOMERS OPEN THE DOOR AND ENTER FIRST.

Whenever possible, they should be the ones to open the door. There are very powerful emotions tied to our tactile senses. Even if you have to unlock the door first, do so and then close it. Stand to the side and let them go first. (If you feel self-conscious or clunky doing this at first, say something like, "This may seem silly, but we are looking at *your* potential home, not mine, and I don't just barge into homes that aren't my own!")

GRAND ENTRANCE TECHNIQUE #4: PAUSE INSIDE FOR FIRST IMPRESSIONS.

Give it just a moment and then ask for their first impressions.

GRAND ENTRANCE TECHNIQUE #5: ASK A SIMPLE BUT POWERFUL CLOSING QUESTION.

"Do you like what you see?" Or, *"How does this entryway feel to you?"* Questions like this become the start of the closing journey.

One more note: What do you do if you have a bad entryway? Let's face it. We like to think every entryway is outstanding, but we know it doesn't always work that way.

Sometimes an entryway lacks drama because of a functional necessity (for example, in a condo with a door that opens to stairs). Sometimes it's just a design flaw. Every home design looks great on paper, but…

In these situations, give different instructions while you are still outside. Instead of saying, *"I want you to take two steps in and stop…"* replace that with, *"I want you to walk to the top of the stairs, stop, and take it all in."* Or, *"I want to start in the kitchen…"*

A CASE STUDY IN IMPROVISATION

Okay, so I've give you some technique tips here but let's agree that there is no such thing as a "one size fits all solution." Let's look at a case study where you would NOT want to follow my advice!

I was doing some troubleshooting at a slow-selling community in Tacoma, Washington when I came across one of the worst entryways I have ever seen.

The front door opened to reveal a toilet, located in a half-bath just to the left of the front door. You couldn't help but see it—it was the first thing you came across and the bathroom door always seemed to be left open. (The fix, by the way: Put a self-closing mechanism on that bathroom door!)

Then, when you opened the door farther, you were met with the landing of a staircase that was placed entirely too close to the front door, giving the appearance of stair rails attacking you.

> "To sing a song is like whispering to a child's ear. It is an art heavily relying on improvisation."
> *Andrea Bocelli*

Between the toilet and the awkward stairs was the formal dining room. On the positive side, a person could use the restroom without missing any dinner conversation!

The ironic aspect of this case study is that the home had an absolutely gorgeous kitchen and great room, with glass on three sides. It was visually stunning, except for the seriously bad taste the entryway left in your mouth.

The solution came by way of a change in presentation technique. I instructed the salespeople to stop on the front porch and say the following:

"We all know that the kitchen is the most important room in the home, and you told me previously that you wanted a great living experience. I want to show you one of the most dramatic kitchen/great room areas I have ever seen. Truly stunning—I think you're going to love it."

I instructed the salespeople to simply lead the charge and blow right past the entry and dining room areas, essentially starting the tour in the dramatic kitchen. Doing so changed everything, and it solved the sales problem.

So what's my point here? Yes, there are best practices that you can use for creating high-impact experiences in most of the homes you show. But you must always think strategically and tactically in each and every situation you encounter.

When you find a home where these tips will hurt you instead of help you, then get strategic and take another approach while still keeping in mind your priorities: customer first, then the home.

APPLICATION QUESTIONS

Ask and answer these questions as you evaluate your experience.

1. Which of the "fails" listed in this chapter have you been guilty of in the past?

2. What new techniques could you employ that would remedy each fail?

3. How would you phrase the home introduction in your own words, making it sound exciting but still conversational?

Write down your commitment to how you will change your approach based on what you have learned.

. . . .

. . . .

. . . .

. . . .

. . . .

CHAPTER 15:

The 5-Point Room-by-Room Experience™

Most home showings take too long. Why? There are a number of reasons actually, but one stands out above all: The salesperson talks too much.

The most effective presentation is an efficient presentation, but feature dumping takes time. Remember that your customer has a limited attention span and operate accordingly.

Spend no more and no less time than what is needed in each room of the home. Like Goldilocks, your goal is to find the "just right" amount of time in each space.

Don't linger in a room that has no value left to discover for the customer. Don't cut a room visit short when the customer is emotionally engaged. Be discerning, *be Goldilocks!*

> Remember that the experience is not about the home, it's about the customer.

So, how exactly *do* you determine that "just right" amount of time to spend in a room? It depends entirely on your customer.

Some rooms require a great deal of time, some very little. It would be so handy if there were a universal, pre-determined formula for the timing of all this, but there isn't.

Remember that the experience is not about the home, it's about the customer. This is why knowing and understanding your customer is so critical. This is where all the work you did in discovery pays off.

REVISITING THE FOUR THINGS YOU MUST KNOW

1) **Motivation:** Why is your customer moving in the first place? *"This house solves your number one problem in that it has four bedrooms: a master, one for each of your kids, and one you can use as a home office."*

2) **Current Dissatisfaction:** What is your customer coming from? *"Check out this huge kitchen with double ovens...it's a great step up from your cramped and dated kitchen, isn't it?"*

3) **Future Promise:** How is your customer envisioning his future in the home? *"Do the size and location of the bathrooms in this house look like they will solve your family's frustrating morning routine you told me about?"*

4) **Family/Stakeholders:** Who gets a say in the decision-making process? *"I know your mom will be living with you in your new home. Do you think she would enjoy this second living area as her own private space?"*

THE 5-POINT ROOM-BY-ROOM EXPERIENCE™

Too many salespeople struggle because they do not know precisely what to do when they enter a new room of the home. They lack a clear and simple strategy for how to get the most out of each area.

This is why I created the 5-Point Room-by-Room Experience. This strategy has proven to be a game-changer for salespeople ranging from the Midwest to the Middle East. The approach is simple, customer-centric, easy to remember, and strategically structured to make the closing step natural and conversational.

You can master this efficient technique if you follow the pattern and practice diligently.

The strategic *process* is the same for each room, but the pattern *sounds* completely different. The difference is based on your customer's responses and the way she engages differently in each room of the home.

Most importantly, the 5-Point Room-by-Room Experience follows our mantra: **Experiential selling is not about the home; it is about the customer.**

WALKING THROUGH THE 5 POINTS

First, let's remember that this is a "Room-by-Room" Experience. You want to repeat these 5 Points in every key room of the home.

So how do you know which rooms are "key"? That's up to your customer. By this time, you should know whether or not a Jack and Jill bathroom is "key" for this home buyer. If it is, well then, use the 5 Point technique for that bathroom just like you would for the glorious gourmet kitchen that might be so important to another home buyer.

ROOM-BY-ROOM POINT #1: ASK FOR FIRST IMPRESSIONS

> This is an incredibly simple but exceedingly powerful technique. When you step into a new area of the home, begin by simply asking, "What do you think?"

You know the saying: You only get one chance to make a first impression. This saying is also true for each room in the home. Your customer will have a first impression of every space. Your job is to allow that to happen and to increase the chances of positive acceptance.

I know that sounds like common sense, but I assure you, this is NOT common practice. Too many salespeople feel the need to start talking right away. ("This is the kitchen.")

The key here is to get the *customer* to talk. All you need is a good trigger question to get that process started.

Variations on "What do you think?":

- *"What are your first impressions of this room?"*
- *"What are you thinking as you see this kitchen for the first time?"*
- *"Right off the bat, tell me how you like this space."*

It is imperative that the customer shares his immediate thoughts. By having him do so, you are helping him be aware of his emotional state. If his first impression of a room is highly positive, he is more likely to love the details as well. (Remember our macro-to-micro approach.) And if he hates it…well, we'll get to that.

ROOM-BY-ROOM POINT #2: ASK FOR SPECIFIC LIKES

Assuming her first impressions are positive, you can then investigate some specific value points.

This is where most salespeople start pointing out features: "Notice the refrigerator." Or worse, this is where salespeople share what *they* like: "I love this fireplace." News flash:

You are not the buyer! Unless you are willing to pull out your checkbook, you do not get a say in what you like about the home.

SOME INSIGHT INTO YOUR BUYER'S MIND

When salespeople start saying what they like or love about a home, it can be a real conversation killer. If a customer doesn't have the chance to say what she likes or dislikes about a feature before the salesperson does, and if she doesn't share the same opinion, that puts her in an awkward spot.

Put yourself in the customer's shoes: You are in the great room and you are about to say, "I'm not sure I like this fireplace surround much at all," but before you get the words out, the enthusiastic salesperson gushes, "I just LOVE this tile around the fireplace!" This leaves you, the customer with two choices: be silent (what most choose) or sound contrary and negative by voicing your opposite opinion.

Uninvited opinions can also plant seeds of doubt and distrust in a customer as he may start to wonder if the salesperson truly understands what he likes and dislikes. The last thing you want to do (in your effort to be positive and enthusiastic) is inadvertently convince your customer that you don't understand him and that he can't trust you to provide him with what he wants!

The far better technique is to ask customers to share their own sense of value. Get them to point out the features that matter to them.

It's a simple request:

* *"What specifically do you like about this space?"*
* *"What jumps out at you?"*
* *"Tell me the things that catch your attention as you look around."*
* *"What else?"*
* *"Keep going…"*

Everything she points out will be valuable because she is telling you what she loves. She had a positive first impression (from step one) but this is when she identifies *why* she likes what she sees. This is her opportunity to identify her personal sense of value. And when *she* identifies the value, then the home truly *is* valuable.

Remember this golden rule for feature dumping: The only time it should take place is when the customer is the one doing it!

ROOM-BY-ROOM POINT #3: DISCUSS LIVABILITY

Having determined what your customer likes, you can move on to how he will live. This will likely be determined by his current dissatisfaction and future promise (see chapter 8).

This is an advanced technique and it is rarely utilized, but it is a technique worth pursuing and mastering.

> "Form follows function —that has been misunderstood. Form and function should be one, joined in a spiritual union."
> *Frank Lloyd Wright*

In *every* key area of the home, ask a livability question:

- *"When you move in, how do you think you will use this entry space? Would it serve as the daily entry for you or as more of a guest entry?"*
- *"Would your piano go in this room? If so, which direction do you want to be facing while you are playing it?"*
- *"You mentioned that it's hard for both of you to work at the same time in your current kitchen…why don't you two whip up an imaginary brunch real quick and see how this kitchen feels when you are both in it."*
- *"I know the lack of storage for your sewing supplies in your current home is frustrating. What do you think of these shelves…are they the right size for how you like to store your material?"*
- *"As you look at this bathroom, can you picture all of your girls in here, getting ready in the morning? What do you think they would say about this space?"*

Using this technique, even the secondary bedrooms become extremely valuable. Think about it. How do you feature dump in a secondary bedroom? *"Umm…. These are the walls, that's the ceiling, there's the floor, that's a window, and you've got a closet over there."* Wow. Captivating.

But when you understand livability, everything changes. You don't talk about the children's bedroom—you talk about the children (using their names!). You don't talk about the hobby room—you talk about the hobby. You don't talk about a place for the piano—you talk about playing the piano.

> As an advanced technique, consider working with the customer to name the rooms as you go along, especially the children's rooms.

Selling livability is about helping the customer personalize a home to her unique living experience.

ROOM-BY-ROOM POINT #4: POINT OUT A FEW SPECIFIC FEATURES (IF NECESSARY)

In this step, you can identify specific value points, if necessary. But how do you know if this step *is* really necessary?

That is entirely up to the buyer. More specifically, this step is determined by how well you know your buyer.

> You want to share the things that are meaningful to your customer. If something doesn't mean anything to your customer, it's not valuable. Period.

Let me say that again. If it isn't meaningful to your customer, it's not valuable.

For example, suppose your customer is currently living in a 40-year-old home and you are showing her something that has been built in the last few years. What would be valuable to her?

- Nine-foot ceilings; certainly higher than what she has now
- Window efficiency; she is probably dealing with insufficient insulation
- Kitchen layout; unless she has remodeled, her current design is likely flawed
- Master bathroom size; not something that was a priority 40 years ago Closet space; in older homes closets are always small (by today's standards)

Ask yourself what will matter to the person standing in front of you right now. Talk about that. And if nothing matters…*don't talk!*

ROOM-BY-ROOM POINT #5: CLOSE ON THE ROOM

Again, this should be common sense, but the practice is far from common. Too many salespeople get anxious about the very word "closing." In this context it is best to think in terms of "acceptance." We are simply asking the customer if he accepts the room as being valuable.

> Closing on each room is not an optional step.
> It is a critical piece of a sound strategy.

This acceptance question is neither heavy nor complex. In fact, you want to keep it very simple and completely conversational:

- *"So, does this room work for you? Excellent, let me show you the…"*
- *"Is this the kitchen you were looking for? Outstanding, let's go see the…"*
- *"Is this the master suite you were hoping to find? Great—let's move on to…"*

BUILDING CONFIDENCE FOR THE CLOSE

Often, salespeople close on a room, a floor plan, or even the entire purchase by asking if the customer can "visualize it."

It sounds like this: "Can you see you and your family enjoying dinner in this formal dining room?" As the salesperson, you may get a "yes" response from the customer, but let me ask you, does that response build your confidence as you move closer to the final close? Not so much.

I can visualize driving a Ferrari, but that doesn't mean I am anywhere close to buying one.

As Jeff suggested above, ask a question that generates a stronger "yes" response. "Does this dining room work for you?" is a great question. It builds your confidence because there is no gray area. Either it works or it doesn't. This question and answer process builds your confidence with each and every room close.

And there you have it—the 5-Point Room-by-Room Experience. Learn it. Memorize it. Use it. Master it. Your presentation will never be the same.

BUT WHAT IF THEY DON'T LIKE IT?

Of course, we are hoping our customers falls in love with what we show them, but we are not naïve about such things. Sometimes it doesn't work out that way.

> "An objection is not a rejection; it is simply a request for more information."
> *Bo Bennett*

The issue at hand is not what they like and dislike. The issue is whether you know about it. You cannot resolve an issue that has not been raised. The 5-Point Room-by-Room Experience brings all issues—positive and negative—to the forefront.

If they don't like the home, or something about the home, follow this pattern for handling objections:

HANDLING OBJECTIONS STEP #1: "TELL ME MORE."

The first thing you need to know is why this is an issue. It doesn't help you when a customer states, "I don't like the fireplace." You need to understand *why* the fireplace presents a problem. Is it aesthetics? Is it function? Is it livability? Is it the finish?

Here are some questions to get your customer to open up:

- *"Tell me more."*
- *"Tell me why."*
- *"Talk to me. What's not working for you?"*

Often, the solution will become clear as they are describing the problem.

HEAT LAMPS AT MCDONALD'S

"Tell me more" is critical because even if you think you understand the buyer's objection, you may not. And sometimes you would never be able to guess what is hanging someone up in a million years.

I was working with a salesperson whose buyer told him she didn't like the recessed lights in the kitchen. Weird, right? He wisely said, "Tell me more about that." Her answer: *"They remind me of the heat lamps at McDonald's and I'm afraid they will get too hot and burn my house down."* Would you have *ever* guessed that? Me neither!

HANDLING OBJECTIONS STEP #2: "HOW IMPORTANT IS THIS TO YOU?"

Sometimes customers voice their displeasure, but it's not that big a deal. If you have asked for elaboration (step one) but that's not getting you anywhere, next determine how important the issue is to the customer. What you need to know is *if this is a deal killer or a deal pauser.*

A simple question like, "Is this something you can live with?" might be all you need to clarify and move on.

> **PRO TIP:**
> Refer back to the macro-to-micro discussion in Chapter 12. You may need to put the objection into perspective for the buyer by reminding her that there are many things *right* with the home. When she thinks of all that's right, is this one imperfect thing something she thinks she would be able to live with?

HANDLING OBJECTIONS STEP #3: "WHAT WOULD YOU DO IF YOU ALREADY LIVED HERE?"

This is an advanced (and very cool) technique, but the approach only works if you are in relational sync with your customer. With this technique, you are taking on the role of "assistant buyer," and in a sense, your customer is the co-salesperson. With this technique, you ask your customer to solve his own problem:

"Let's assume for just a moment that you had already moved in and you had to make it work. What would you do?"

For example, if the customers are struggling with a backyard that they deem too small, instead of rushing to offer a barrage of solutions, you could simply ask (while standing in the backyard), *"Mr. and Mrs. Buyer, if you already lived here, how would you design this space to make it work?"*

You will be amazed at how creative buyers can get at solving their own problems. When they come up with the solution themselves, they will always be happier than if the idea came from you.

If the problem is unsolvable, go back to point number two. But you'll find that customers can be amazingly creative when they like a home.

> You are not trying to sell the perfect
> home to your customer;
> you are trying to sell the best home.

Finally, keep in mind that there is no such thing as a perfect home. It simply does not exist. Everyone compromises. You, me, Bill Gates, *everyone!*

APPLICATION

There are no questions for this chapter. But you do have a very important assignment: PRACTICE! But do so in these stages:

1. Write out some sample verbiage for communicating with your customers in each of the five points.

2. Practice saying what you wrote out loud (very important) over and over again, so you can get comfortable with the flow of the wording.

3. Find a practice partner and go through the 5-Point Room-by-Room Experience five times in five different areas of a home. See how the strategy stays the same but the conversation is totally different as you move along.

4. Commit to performing the 5-Point Room-by-Room Experience with five successive customers. When it comes to skill development, the worst thing you can do is to try something one time. Commit to doing this repeatedly and then master the technique.

CHAPTER 16:

Experiencing Key Living Areas

Now that you understand how to use the 5-Point Room-by-Room Experience in any room of the home, let's narrow our discussion to some very specific areas.

> While you want to be thinking about some general ideas for each area of the home, you must always keep in mind that the experience in any given room is completely up to your buyer.

Don't get caught dictating the way *you* think a room should be used. If your customer wants a pool table in the formal dining room—awesome!

If she wants to put a trampoline in the living room with the high ceiling—well, go for it!

PLAYING THE NAME GAME WITH YOUR HOME BUYERS

Below you will see a list of spaces typically found in homes and ideas on how to best connect with your buyers in each of them.

However, it is important to understand that these labels are here only to help you, the reader, understand the spaces we are referencing. When you are showing a home to your buyers, I encourage you to NOT use the labels below, but instead ask your buyers how *they* would name the spaces.

For example, I don't know anyone who refers to the secondary rooms in their home as "secondary bedrooms" or "bedroom #1, #2, or #3". Do you ever say, "Honey, can you take this to bedroom #2?"

Of course not, your bedroom #2 has a personal label which you have given it. You call it "Claire's room" or "the guest Room." Let the buyer name the spaces and then use their room titles throughout the experience.

FORMAL LIVING ROOM

The modern trend is moving away from the formal living room, but for decades this space was considered essential. In ages past, this room was the showpiece of the home—a decorative statement of sorts.

As a young man I recall my friends' mothers telling me in very stern tones that I was *not* permitted to sit on their living room furniture. The living room was adults-only territory and it went hand-in-hand with cordials, pipes, and well-groomed grownups. (Think: *Mad Men* and coordinated tea and coffee sets served on a tray. There is a reason a "coffee table" is called just that!)

Because using a formal living room in a formal way has ceased to be the norm, today's home buyer is faced with an interesting question when considering a home which has a formal living room: How will she use the space? Increasingly, we see a great degree of creativity when answering that question.

Some customers see the formal space as a negative. They don't believe they will use it but they have to pay for it. This is where the savvy sales professional can provide great value by facilitating creative brainstorming about how the customers might use this space to enrich their unique lifestyle.

> "Creativity requires the courage to let go of certainties."
> *Erich Fromm*

The answer to this question harkens back to the customer's current dissatisfaction and future promise. Start by contrasting what this room offers compared to your customer's present space so that you have a frame of reference to work from. Then consider what is wrong with her current home and how the formal living room space might present a creative solution.

For example, a couple with three small children might not see the need for a formal living room, but with a creative screen in place to hide the clutter, the space might make an excellent play area. In formal living rooms all around the world you can find a Little Tikes™ play set or beanbags in place of a coffee table. It works!

That said, selling the formal living room as exactly that might be just the ticket for the home buyer who is looking to upgrade his lifestyle. In this case, take your customer on a mental journey, picturing festive social gatherings and personal relaxation in the lush environs of this upscale space. Fill in the imagery with a description of sensory details: fresh flowers, a glass of wine at the end of a long day, and classy art and furniture.

FORMAL DINING ROOM

Like the formal living room, the formal dining room has seen a decrease in popularity of late. Yet for many, this remains an absolute must-have.

The interesting thing about the formal dining room is that it is rarely used, but when people *do* think about it, they recall warm memories of extended family gatherings, holidays, and special events. This room represents tremendous memory potential and

The interesting thing about the formal dining room is that it is rarely used, but when people do think about it, they recall warm memories of extended family gatherings, holidays, and special events.

perhaps more cherished times than any other space. In many ways, the formal dining room is the ultimate example of buying the experience.

For buyers who do not have strong dining room memories or expectations, you can take the same approach that we discussed for the formal living room. The formal dining room can be re-purposed as a music area, a craft room, or even a space for that long desired pool table. Hey, there are no rules.

The customer needs to know that he can do whatever he likes with the spaces. The architect who designed the home has no say in how it lives! It is your job to make sure your customer knows and feels this freedom.

However, if the formal dining room is to be used as such, you *must* sell it based on life scenes. Dr. Daniel Kahneman refers to these future moments as "anticipated memories."

> The role of the salesperson is to take the customer into that anticipated memory—the future experiences they will enjoy in that space.

Paint the picture with emotional language, and be sure the customer has a strong sense of ownership and connection to the imagery you create. (If you are picturing the famous Normal Rockwell scene of an extended family gathered around the table for a Thanksgiving feast, you are right on track!)

FAMILY ROOM / GREAT ROOM

For most people, the family room represents the space where real life is lived. Important conversations will take place here as will fun and laughter. Kids will learn a love for reading in this space. Friends will spend hours of time just hanging out on the family room sofas. And yes, a whole lot of television will be watched.

The great room is an experiential room, so the strategy should be obvious: *Get your customer experiencing the space.*

> It makes absolutely no sense to walk through a family room without sitting on the sofa, because when in a great room do people *not sit on the sofa?*

It makes absolutely no sense to walk through a family room without sitting on the sofa, because when in a great room do people *not sit on the sofa?*

Think about it. When was the last time you stood on the outskirts of your own family room and just assessed the space? "Yep, there's my family room. I paid extra for that ceiling fan, and I remember the battle over the flooring. Ah, the memories." No! No! No! The great room is appreciated from a seated position. So get your customer sitting.

What are most people doing when sitting in their family room? Watching television, of course. The average American spends three hours per day watching television, most of that time from his sofa.

Given this fact, I suggest mentally placing the television *first*. Do this by simply asking your customer where his TV will go.

Many salespeople first ask about sofa placement. I disagree. Figure out where the television goes and everything else will fall into place. It is difficult to picture your TV without picturing your sofa, and along with it, the relaxed feeling you have when you get to kick back and watch your shows in the peace and privacy of your own home.

Getting your customer to imagine this feeling is your goal when you ask him where his TV will go. It's a short journey from the question to the feeling, but you are the only one who can book that trip for your buyer!

"DOING" INSTEAD OF "IMAGINING"

When discussing livability with your buyer in a specific space, any time you are about to say, "Can you picture yourself...?" ask yourself if instead you can actually have the buyer do it!

For example, instead of saying "Can you picture yourself sitting here reading while still being able to see your kids playing in the backyard?" have her sit down as if she is actually reading and have her look out into the backyard.

Doing is much more powerful than imagining.

PUT YOUR HOME BUYER "INSIDE" THE MOMENT

One of the new home salespeople we work with shared this brilliant idea:

His model homes featured real TVs connected via an Apple TV appliance, so he asks his customers what their favorite show or sports team is. Once he has them in the family room, he has them pick "their spot" on the couch and he then plays a YouTube clip of their favorite show or team.

Talk about creating an experience!

KITCHEN:

Many studies have found that a woman's favorite room in the home is the kitchen. But what about the men? What is their favorite room? Believe it or not, the answer is also the kitchen.

Today's kitchen represents so much more than just a food preparation area. The kitchen is command central in most homes these days. Schedules are made and coordinated in the kitchen, bills are paid, homework is done, home businesses are managed… And yes, gourmet meals (and frozen dinners) are prepped and often eaten in this space.

This is such an exciting space to share the future experience…when it's done right. That said, the kitchen is the most difficult room to show effectively. There is so much going on, so many features, so many things to talk about. It can quickly become overwhelming.

> Everyone has a different idea of how a kitchen is best utilized. *What is it for the customer standing in front of you?*

The key to starting your presentation strong is establishing top-level emotional engagement with the kitchen. If you get dragged into details too soon, you will only confuse your customer. Remember our macro-to-micro approach. Start with the first impression question from our 5-Point Room-by-Room Experience to ensure the customer is emotionally engaged.

Before you have much of a chance to go macro, customers often start asking a lot of detail questions. Your best strategy: Don't answer…yet. It makes no sense to talk about the micro until you have gained agreement on the macro. In fact, once your customer likes the kitchen on the top level, those detail questions will be easier to answer.

Try this approach:

"Those are all excellent questions and I will get to each of them. But the details don't really mean much if you don't like the kitchen as a whole. Take a step back and give me your big-picture impression of this kitchen."

From there, you can get into life scene pictures. Everyone has a different idea of how a kitchen is best utilized. What is it for the customer standing in front of you? The more vividly he can imagine his "anticipated memories," the more ownership he will take in the home.

One other thing about showing the kitchen: There are two key components that all customers have strong opinions about in regard to their dream kitchen: countertops and cabinet space. Be sure to highlight both of these elements, preferably with data.

> Quote the linear footage of countertop space. Count the cabinets and drawers and share that number with your buyer. It will always sound impressive and it will give the customer a memory point for these critical elements.

Finally, do not neglect point three in the 5-Point Room-by-Room Experience: livability questions. These are critical. *"When you imagine yourself living with this kitchen, what does that look like? Paint the scene for me. What is happening here"?*

When the customer answers these types of questions, she will go through the important process of trying the kitchen on for size.

KITCHEN LIVABILITY TIPS

1. **Ask "Who is where, doing what?"**
   When discussing livability, you want to move beyond yes or no questions like *"Can you imagine preparing Thanksgiving dinner for your family in this kitchen?"*

   Instead, ask a more engaging question that gets customers talking. For example: *"If this kitchen were yours, where would each of your family members be and what would each of them be doing in preparation for your Thanksgiving feast?"*

2. **Change the Customer's Perspective**
   As human beings, we have a unique ability to see things through other people's eyes. Let's say you are talking with a husband who is doing the preliminary work before his wife comes out to view the home.

When standing in the kitchen, you can change his perspective by saying, "Walk through the kitchen and see it through your wife's eyes. Then tell me how she would compare this kitchen to her current one."

MASTER SUITE

The master suite might be the most difficult room in the home when it comes to selling the experience. This room is, of course, highly personal. And I'm not just talking about the obvious insinuation here.

This room is where we are private, personal, and vulnerable. Think for a moment about what you look like when you are sleeping, sick, or when you first roll out of bed. Get the not-so-flattering picture?

For this reason, the master suite experience is really about the mental move-in. And that is centered around two primary elements.

First, get the top-level opinion. Go back to step one in the 5-Point Room-by-Room technique and ask for their first impression.

Second, place the furniture. The placement of their furniture is a safe way to accomplish a mental move-in.

> When showing the master bedroom you really just want to be responsive to the customer's emotions. Don't try to overreach here by painting life pictures for your customer. Let the customer do that.

SECONDARY BEDROOMS

For many, the secondary bedrooms are something of an afterthought. Accordingly, the presentation usually sounds something like this:

"This is bedroom two. And over here is bedroom three. Let's move on."

Think about it. I challenge you to feature-dump in a secondary bedroom. *"This room features a floor and a ceiling and some walls and a closet, a door and a window. Did I mention the outlets?"*

It doesn't need to be this way. All you need to do to enrich the secondary bedrooms' experience is sell the future experience and the anticipated memories. When you understand how each room will be used, you can introduce a mental picture.

> With the cooperation of your customers, go through and name each room. Ask them how they will refer to each room after they have moved in.

Here's a tip to help you do that effectively. With the cooperation of your customers, go through and name each room. Ask them how they will refer to each room after they have moved in. Their responses will sound something like this:

- *"This will be Lisa's room."*
- *"I'll call this the junk room."*
- *"This is our hobby room."*
- *"This is where my man cave goes."*

In each instance the customer is establishing ownership of that space.

One last technique tip: Don't go into a small room with a customer. Three full-grown adults in a 10x10 space will make such a room look really, really small.

> There is no reason why you cannot stand in the hall and peek in while your customer experiences the room first-hand.

GARAGE

Talk about an after-thought—the garage is almost like a throwaway to many salespeople. Yet when you think about how important garage space is when it comes to day-to-day living, you understand that the importance of this space *cannot* be understated.

> "The more storage you have, the more stuff you accumulate."
> *Alexis Stewart*

The fact is that we live in a society where it is quite normal to accumulate stuff (aka junk). It has to go somewhere, and for many people the very idea of putting two cars in a two-car garage is laughable. That would never be their intention based on their need to store their stuff. So, great! Here's where all the stuff goes.

Others are all about their cars, and the garage functions as a kind of very large jewelry box. If this is the kind of customer you are dealing with, the garage conversation is not about the garage at all—it is about his pride and joy.

The key is to let the customer spend as much time in the garage as he needs to. You don't need to oversell this space, but you don't want to neglect it either.

One other tip about the garage experience: Find creative storage. As I mentioned, for many people the garage is where all their miscellaneous junk is stored.

Work with your customer on how to multiply space. Is there a nook somewhere that will accommodate shelves? Does the garage have a little extra width for a workbench? Can you hang platform shelves from the ceiling to store skis, decorations, etc.?

BEWARE OF GENDER BIAS!

I sometimes find that we falsely assume that the garage is a "man's" space, something the ladies wouldn't be much interested in. This couldn't be farther from the truth and can even come off as offensive if we say something like *"I bet the garage is really important to your husband, huh?"*

A garage can make everyone feel safe as they enter the home and close the door behind them before exiting their car in the evening. It is extremely handy to be in a covered space when loading or unloading kids, dogs, groceries, etc.

Additionally, women often use the garage as much as men for crafting projects, furniture painting, small business storage, etc. As with all spaces of the home, we should never assume who will use what space based on gender.

BACKYARD

Like the great room, the backyard represents a significant lifestyle consideration. The backyard experience is a powerful mental trigger that takes us back to our earliest childhood memories. Barbeques, birthday parties, hanging out on a warm summer evening, romping with a new puppy—you get the picture.

Selling the backyard is really about the life scenes. And once again we go back to the recurring question: How well do you know your customers? How do they use their outdoor space now? How emotional are they about that? Do they envision scenes that include large groups of people and hilarious laughter or more personal moments with peace and quiet?

When selling the backyard experience you want to get your customer very engaged. Don't ever show the backyard just by standing at the sliding glass door and looking out. Walk to the end of the yard and look back at the home.

> Look at the yard space from various angles. Have your customer sit down, if possible, and really take in the space.

Look at the yard space from various angles. Have your customer sit down, if possible, and really take in the space.

You'll also want to show the future possibilities of the backyard. Perhaps a pool will be in order when the kids get a little older. There might not be a family dog today, but down the road? What would small fruit trees, planted today, look like in five years?

Explore your home buyer's backyard vision instead of just stating its size.

> The measurements of a backyard may never change, but the possibilities are endless.

SPECIAL PLACES

Every home has its special little corners, those spaces that add character and provide future memories. Pay close attention to these often tiny spaces. For example:

- *How might you use this closet under the stairs?*
- *What can you put on that shelf above the entryway?*
- *Is there artwork or furniture that would work in this alcove?*
- *Where does the dog sleep?*
- *Where can I keep my collection of books (or plates or dolls)?*
- *What is the best corner in the home for my reading chair?*
- *Where can I place my grandmother's armoire?*

MAKING IT MEMORABLE

Here is a tip to make sure the most significant areas of a home will make a lasting impression in the buyer's mind: Take pictures as you go along.

> If the customers see something they really like,
> snap a quick picture and send it to them later.

This will extend their emotional attachment to the home and reconnect them to what they loved so much. It also helps distinguish one home from another and helps you stand out in your home buyer's mind and emotions.

APPLICATION EXERCISE: PUTTING IT INTO PRACTICE

We have covered a whole lot of technique in this chapter, too much to act on all at once. I encourage you to go back and scan this chapter right this minute, looking for the most prominent application ideas.

Identify five action items that you can work on right away. Then prioritize that list by impact. Determine which techniques will have the strongest impact on your buyer's experience and start there:

Action Item	Priority	Impact On My Buyer

Once you have begun to incorporate that technique into your presentation, go back and layer in another. In no time at all you will have transformed your entire presentation!

. . . .

. . . .

. . . .

. . . .

. . . .

. . . .

. . . .

. . . .

. . . .

. . . .

. . . .

. . . .

. . . .

. . . .

. . . .

. . . .

. . . .

. . . .

CHAPTER 17:

Wrapping Up the Experience

We all make decisions by way of mental shortcuts. We are forever on a quest to keep things as easy as possible.

Psychologists call this "cognitive fluency" and there is no escaping it—it's how we are hardwired. In a nutshell, cognitive fluency has to do with how easy or difficult it is to think about something and how that ease or strain affects us.

When something is simple to understand—a process, a product, a conversation—our stress is lessened and the simplicity of whatever we are faced with makes it easier for us to accept. In short, easy equals right.

> "In character, in manner, in style, in all things, the supreme excellence is simplicity."
> *Henry Wadsworth Longfellow*

This mental processing is accomplished largely on a subconscious level. We often call it a "gut feeling" and it is a very real factor in our decision-making.

Now think back to our discussion about "emotional altitude," a measurement of the positive energy customers carry throughout the purchase process. When they possess a higher level of emotional altitude, they experience a greater degree of cognitive fluency, which translates into a more simple buying decision.

> Customers want to make purchase decisions when their emotional altitude peaks.

For example, think about the purchase of a wedding dress; the bride-to-be says "I'll take it," often through tears. Remember the last time you bought a really cool big-screen television? You were stoked, right? Can you feel the emotional altitude in those moments?

I'm thinking of the last time I took a car for a test drive. I was fairly giddy about the idea of owning that car (although I admit I did not want to show that positive energy to the salesperson). The test drive was a time of high emotional altitude.

But then the salesperson said, "Let's go back and crunch some numbers." Ugh! Talk about a buzzkill! The thought of going back to a cubicle to pound out a deal completely deflated my emotional altitude. Thanks, salesperson, thanks a lot!

THE EMOTIONAL CRESCENDO

> Making it easy for customers to purchase the home of their dreams should be our objective.

They are most likely to do this when they just plain feel good.

Try to picture the sales process as an emotional crescendo. The positive energy should continually build as you get closer to the culmination of the process: a purchase decision. You want your customer to make this decision at a time of high emotional altitude.

WHERE TO END

> Here is one technique that will help promote emotional altitude. Make sure the last stop in the experience is always the space that meant the most to the customers.

Wrap up the conversation by heading to the room that really resonated with them. It's a simple technique on your part: *"Let's take one more look at…"*

Trust me; they will want to go with you, because they know deep down this is where their positive sentiment was the strongest. Revisiting their favorite space reconnects them to that positive emotion, and their emotional altitude peaks.

"John, Maria, I know the backyard view was really the best thing about this home for you. Let's take one more look at it, shall we?" Very simple, but very powerful.

WRAPPING IT UP – THE SUMMARY CLOSE

You've walked back to the area that means the most to the customers, and this is precisely where we will culminate the sale while the customers are at their emotional peak. The high emotions make for cognitive fluency, and that increases the joy of making a decision.

Don't leave that space without a closing question!

The best possible approach is to use the Summary Close. If you followed the 5-Point Room-by-Rom Experience carefully, you have already closed in every significant room or area of the home. This is when that diligent work pays off.

> You've walked back to the area that means the most to the customers, and this is precisely where we will culminate the sale while the customers are at their emotional peak.

To use the Summary Close you will simply revisit everything that they have already agreed to. In so doing, you are leveraging the principle of commitment and consistency.

In short, people don't argue with themselves. Your customers have already told you (well, more importantly, they told themselves) that they loved each of the different rooms in the home. Now we simply revisit all those minor decisions and roll them up into a final decision.

It sounds something like this:

> *"John and Maria, it's been really fun for me to show you this home. Clearly it has a lot going on that works for you. The kitchen is a significant upgrade from what you have now and seems to be perfect for your growing family. The master suite allows you to get the king-sized bed you've always wanted. The kids have picked out their bedrooms and seem to be happy with them. You said the bonus room makes for a perfect retreat space. And, of course, the backyard is everything you had hoped for. It looks like everything works. Would you like to make it yours?"*

> Note that I did not ask again for confirmation
> on all the different areas. I simply restated
> what they had already told me.

I'm not being manipulative here—if they hated a part of the home, I would know it.

APPLICATION EXERCISE: CRAFTING YOUR SUMMARY CLOSE

The Summary Close is arguably the most effective closing technique I know, because it is based entirely on a partnership with the customer. But understand that this technique does not come naturally. It requires a great deal of practice. And let's face it; if there was ever a time to be silky smooth in your delivery, this would most definitely be it.

Think of the last person you sold a home to. If you had used the Summary Close with that customer, what would it have sounded like? Write it out in the space below:

. . . .

. . . .

. . . .

. . . .

. . . .

. . . .

. . . .

. . . .

Now commit to practicing the Summary Close over and over again. Practice until you are sick of your own voice, then do it twenty times more. Trust me on this: When you get the approach right, you will change your customer's world!

CHAPTER 18:

Vision Into Action

Well, you made it. We've come to the end of our journey together. But this is only the *start of your* journey with your customers.

The time you have invested in reading this book is for naught unless you diligently apply what you have learned, all in the service of an incredible experience for your home buyer.

Allow me to share some specific ideas on how to do that. Consider this a "Where do we grow from here?" discussion.

STEP #1: APPLY

> Learning something different is cool. *Doing* something differently is transformative.

As people who work in sales, we are prone to take action. This is good! It's not only about applying what you have learned—that's just the first step. It's really about creating new habits. Dan Sullivan, founder of Strategic Coach, suggests that *when we think we need more discipline in our lives, what we really need is better habits.*

> "Energy and persistence conquer all things."
> Benjamin Franklin

Let that truth sink in for a minute.

Let me encourage you to adopt one new technique per day, every day for the next month. This is a good way to go step by step through the book.

Or, you can identify the growth opportunities that mean the most to you and create a schedule for implementing them, one at a time.

Start simple. Set yourself up for success. As you gain mastery, you will gain confidence as well.

STEP #2: REPEAT

> It's not enough to try a new technique once. In fact, trying a sales technique only one time is a supremely bad idea. It can be downright dangerous.

When we attempt a technique that we have not mastered, we end up paying a price in the form of discomfort at the least, and embarrassment at the most. Beware: Our first response to perceived failure is not "I need to work on that." No, your brain will instead send you this message loud and clear: *"Don't do that again!"*

I want to encourage you to do the work of repetition by yourself or with a practice partner. It is crucial to get new language, phrasing, timing, etc. down solid before trying it with a customer.

Mastering new techniques without a real live home buyer standing in front of you will build your confidence and enable you to interact naturally and comfortably with your customer.

Remember this critically important truth:

> The destination called mastery lies on a road called repetition.

There are no shortcuts!

Here's one more pro tip for you: Record your practice sessions. You can dramatically decrease the duration of your learning curve if you listen to yourself and make changes accordingly. Hearing yourself externally (vs. the sound of your voice in your own head) provides a quick and high-quality brand of assessment. Try it! (And yes, no one likes the sound of his or her own voice. Get over it!)

STEP #3: ENJOY A MENTAL SNACK

I have several books I keep around as "mental snacks." This can be one of those books for you.

The regular refueling of your brain is critical to your success. Snacking on the bite-sized bits

> The sooner you apply a lesson, the greater the chance you will actually use it in your sales presentation.

(which you have highlighted, underlined, circled) that are most relevant to you is like caffeine for your brain: invigorating and motivating.

The key is to apply what you learn right away. The sooner you apply a lesson, the greater the chance you will actually use it in your sales presentation. Book "snacks" are like that cup of water a runner grabs in the middle of a marathon. Chug it down and *keep going!*

STEP #4: JOURNAL

I have been journaling for over fifteen years. I take great delight in re-reading my thoughts from long ago and marking the progress I have made in my life.

> When we are learning something new, we feel insecure and frustrated. Write those thoughts and feelings down.

You will find that as you conquer your discomforts, your confidence will increase. Soon you will be journaling your successes.

Journaling has a way of cementing what we learn, but it also serves as a self-accountability tool. We are more likely to *actually* do things when we write them down. (Good intentions are the burial grounds of countless would-be actions!) Journal to learn better and to keep yourself moving forward.

STEP #5: TEACH

They say the best way to learn something is to teach it. Consider volunteering to teach what you have learned. This could be at a future sales meeting (your sales manager will likely be happy to hand over a portion of the meeting to you) or in the form of volunteering as a mentor for new salespeople.

> We learn things at a far deeper level when we know we will be teaching whatever we are learning.

Quite simply, you will learn more than your student(s) when you commit to teaching.

STEP #6: RE-READ

You will go stale at some point. I promise. It's inevitable. We learn something new and practice until we are comfortable and then…we plateau. The learning curve becomes a flat, horizontal line. Don't get thrown off by this reality. Expect it. Know that this is what it means to be human and work to constantly push your own learning curve forward.

When you feel staleness creeping in, consider it your cue to re-read. The good news is that you will discover entirely new things on your second or third read of this book.

> Your mind will respond to your new need each time you re-read. It's how we are wired.

I have read the Bible many times in my life. I am constantly amazed at how I learn new things every time I read it—as if every time is the first time. This is a reflection of how the brain works. Remember the adage: When the student is ready, the teacher will appear.

A WORD OF GRATITUDE

On behalf of Amy O'Conner, Ryan Taft and all the people who had a hand in putting this book together, thanks so much for honoring us with your investment of time and diligent study. It was a joy for us to write this book, but it is all only abstract until a sales professional reads it and lives it.

Our hope is that this book will advance your presentation to an entirely new level. Further, we want you to comprehend the gravity of what you have just read. You do something really special—you help people accomplish a lifelong dream. You are called to do it in a way that is truly enjoyable for your customer and yourself.

You are not just selling a home; you are building the foundation of an incredible life experience.

You are changing someone's world.